Jean-Claude Biver

The Wizard of Swiss Watchmaking

Jean-Claude Biver

The Wizard of Swiss Watchmaking

Interviews with Gérard Lelarge

orell füssli Verlag

2. Edition 2019

Orell Füssli Verlag, www.ofv.ch

Cover design: Hauptmann & Kompanie Werbeagentur, Zürich, using a motif from © Viktor Chlad
Printing: CPI books GmbH, Leck

ISBN 978-3-280-05683-7

The National Library of Germany has recorded this publication in the National Bibliography of Germany; detailed bibliographical data is available on the Internet under www.dnb.de.

FSC www.fsc.org
MIX
Papier aus verantwortungsvollen Quellen
FSC® C083411

Contents

Foreword

Meeting The Man

I first met the president and CEO of Hublot – and future president of the watchmaking division of LVMH – at the Wine Business Club, when he was invited to speak about the marriage of gold and rubber.

Jean-Claude Biver ... A master watchmaker who not only values the image of the Swiss luxury industry but also makes cheese, not to sell but to give away at his press conferences everywhere from New York to Tokyo, Beijing to Lausanne ... A big boss who, with a great gale of laughter, explains that he bought Blancpain with his friend Jacques Piguet in 1981 for 22 000 Swiss francs (about 21 000 euros) and sold it for 60 million ten years later ... A lover and collector of the great wines who has all the vintages of Château d'Yquem since 1811 .... A sexagenarian with a sparkling irrepressible smile, delighted to be both father and grandfather ... An executive whose management principles have remarkable effects on the sales, turnover and profitability of the companies he runs ... A leader who resurrected Blancpain in 1982, turned Omega around during the 1990s, and put Hublot into orbit in 2004 ... A leader who took TAG Heuer into the future with the creation of the connected watch.

At the end of his short speech, I elbow my way forward to exchange a few words with him. I give him my card. He gives me his! I write to him to explain my idea to write his biography. A few days later, I receive a card covered with the large black, elegant and forceful letters of his, distinctive, sloping handwriting. Then an e-mail sent at 5:33 pm. An appointment is fixed at a large Paris hotel at 11:15. At 11 am, his assistant sends me an SMS: "Monsieur Biver is sincerely sorry. He will be a quarter of an hour late. How many big bosses would show such respect towards someone they barely know?"

Jean-Claude Biver puts his hand in his briefcase and brings out my two page proposal. He okays the whole thing. I then bring out the "Proust questionnaire" for him to answer later. "Why later? Let's do it now." Clearly the project excites him. And so begin several months of meetings in Paris and in Nyon near Geneva where the Hublot factory is located.

I took great pleasure in these meetings and the writing of this book. I am proud to believe that JCB also enjoyed these exchanges which enabled him, to describe his unique journey with all his characteristic passion and enthusiasm.

Enjoy discovering – or rediscovering – an original, compelling and unmissable actor on the stage of today's luxury watch business. A true magician of Swiss watchmaking.

Gérard Lelarge

1

"Passion makes everything possible"

Finding your path

From the steam engine to the Swiss watch

Gérard Lelarge: You define yourself as a man of passion and conviction. Primarily a man of passion. In 1975, you found your path: watchmaking. How did it become your main passion?

Jean-Claude Biver: Very simply: one day my friend Jacques Piguet showed me the mechanism of his watch, and looking at its wheels and arbors I rediscovered a much-loved toy of my childhood: a steam engine. Jacques said to me: "You seem to be passionate, you should work in watchmaking." He was right. There are indeed similarities between my treasured steam engine and the watch industry; they both have mechanisms, wheels, pivots, axles, motors. Moving from the steam engine to the watch is nothing more than moving from a child's toy to an adult's toy. A child is never bored with a good toy; so when one grows up one should not be bored with an adult's toy either. The watch became the toy of my adulthood and watchmaking my passion.

I often explain to young people: passion is not always something you are born with. You must seek it out. And when you find it, your work will not only be your livelihood, but your passion. You will then find your path and you will leave a lasting impression of yourself.

You think leaving a trace of yourself is essential?

Yes, to be precise everyone should leave two traces in life: a professional trace and a trace of love. They are essential because they give a reason to live. On the day that I am no longer here, I want to leave these two traces: among my family, my friends and my professional circle.

Your passion is to innovate, to create. You have succeeded in making your passion your profession; Which is a very appreciable "PLUS".

Making one's passion a profession is more than a 'plus' it is actually a huge privilege. For me it is not a case of 'work during the week and passion at weekends'. My job is my passion. So for me, every day is a weekend

Mister Five-Ten

Carlos Ghosn is often called "Mister Seven-Eleven" because he was in the office from 7 am until 11 pm. In concrete terms, how is a "typical day" of Jean-Claude Biver structured?

I get up between 4 and 5 o'clock, sometimes earlier … The first thing I do is check my e-mails: every night, between 10 pm, when I leave my computer, and 4 or 5 am, I have received about 100 emails. I reply immediately. My day has begun. At eight o'clock I leave for the factory in Nyon and arrive in my office at half-past eight. You describe Carlos Ghosn as "Mister Seven-Eleven" I am rather "Mister Five-Ten". (Great burst of laughter.)

I can work fifteen or twenty hours a day, three hundred and sixty days a year; I never feel like I am working. Someone passionate never stops. To invest yourself completely in a project is not work if what you do is your passion. And I am lucky enough that the this is the case with me. I can log off for a few hours, but not a fortnight. I live with my passion all the time.

Some believe that excessive personal commitment and work-addiction that becomes work-bulimia may lead to flawed decision-making. Do you share that view and what safeguards need to be put in place?

You cannot do it alone. Like all enthusiasts, I am bulimic when it comes to working. But my management style is based on a systematic search for consensus. I try not to impose anything, I prefer to share my ideas. I do not want to implement them without involving my team. It is always the team that wins. Hence the importance of knowing how to surround yourself with capable staff. The entrepreneur is a conductor: he cannot be the best pianist as well as the best guitarist.

Passion may be essential to success, but do you think there is the danger of it affecting your judgement?

One should not be afraid of passion. If from time to time there are excesses of enthusiasm, these are compensated by all the positive things passion brings. Passion enriches so much that one can live with its occasional excesses.

Another essential passion for you: sport, more exactly the sports you practice regularly. You were a Luxembourg university ski champion, you have run the New York marathon, you cycle regularly – several thousand kilometres a year – you ski, you sail …

For many years, I was a keen hiker and cycled an average of 10 000 kilometres per year. Today I do 10 hours of mountain biking per week, often very early in the morning. I believe that any entrepreneur is a sportsman, not necessarily in a physical sense, but in the mind. Being athletic means living a healthy lifestyle, having discipline and endurance, as well as learning from your defeats. Sport is an extraordinary means of education and personal development since it teaches you to know yourself, to discipline yourself, to turn failures into successes.

2

"Share, Respect and Forgive"

Living your ethics day to day

Gérard Lelarge: As we have seen you are a man of passion, but also of conviction. Your behaviour is guided by what you call your "three commandments": sharing, respecting, forgiving. How do these three commandments – which you have written with your wife's lipstick on the mirror of your children's bathroom – translate into your daily life as a big boss?

Jean-Claude Biver: My first commandment is sharing. When you share your doubts and even your failures with your team, you strengthen your ties with them. A boss who says to his team: "I have doubts" or "I was mistaken" is a boss we want to love. My second commandment is respect. By respecting your suppliers, you make them partners, who will therefore be ready to cooperate more and come to you with new ideas. Finally, my third commandment, the most important, is forgiveness. We must forgive errors. Above all, do not paralyze the employee. He who knows that he will always be understood and forgiven for the fault he has committed will want to tackle new challenges. Error is inherent in human activity: one cannot wait to be 100 % sure to decide. If we wait, we decide too late: the train has already left the station! In business, you have to be visionary; vision implies uncertainty and therefore the risk of being mistaken.

Through your "three commandments" you seek to be the same man at home and at work. I imagine that these rules of life are a source of harmony, therefore essential if you are to flourish.

My life is aligned and harmonious. If I were to change my job, I would not be in harmony. A man who is not in harmony is a weak man; strength comes from harmony, and harmony can only come from love. Sharing, respecting and forgiving are commandments based in love. They are easy to understand because of direct, daily application.

On the subject of conviction, what is your position with regard to religion?

Religion is a necessity: man needs reference points. In the past, ethics were taught by parents, religion and school; these three actors converged to bring values and principles to children. Today, it is believed, in my opinion wrongly, that this is no longer the role of school. For their part, parents do not always play their full role: one parent in two is divorced and most women work and are less available for their children. Finally, I think that religion no longer plays its role completely because it has not adapted enough to the language of youth: too often it speaks as if we were still living in the Middle Ages.

3

"First, Different and Unique"

Becoming and remaining a leader

Inventing new paths

Gérard Lelarge: Now to deal directly with the world of business, always being "first, different and unique" is for you essential.

Jean-Claude Biver: I made this my slogan, but it is probably as old as the world. For my part, I have adopted this "truism" as a rule that must absolutely be respected, in order to define our strategy. I think that if you are first, different and unique, you do not normally lose. This rule forces us to search obsessively for new ideas, which otherwise would not have come to mind. I will give you just one example: Hublot entered football in 2005, whereas, a priori, this sport could seem far removed from the values of a luxury company.

For you it is simple: "no innovation, no life; No innovation, no future." Innovation is necessary to survive. It is the best antidote to crisis.

"No innovation, no future" is perfectly true, but in Swiss watchmaking, you also need to add: "no tradition, no future". It is imperative that we innovate within tradition, and above all that we must not be satisfied with just repeating it. Repeating tradition is the role of a museum, not a business. Tradition must be the basis on which innovation is built. Combining the past and the future, tradition and innovation is the "art of fusion" that characterizes Hublot.

Beyond Hublot there are the innovations of TAG Heuer that you have led for three years and Zenith of which you took daily management in 2017.

At the end of 2015 TAG Heuer created its first connected watch and in early 2017 Zenith launched a new version of its famous El Primero movement, first launched in in 1969, with a cut-out dial revealing the workings of its movement. This with a display at 1/10th of a second!

I like to do things differently, to clear new paths, to conquer new territories. Breaking away and constantly innovating enables us to progress. That's what I have done systematically throughout my career. If I have succeeded it is because I knew how to be different and because I had the courage to do things differently. The message to young people is clear: not only to have passion, but to dare to innovate and have the courage to make a mistake.

In your opinion, we must go beyond what we have learned and break out of the boundaries that restrict us.

School is important but it can tend to format us. Don't follow the school book to the letter. Sometimes I even say: "do the opposite of what it teaches!" Do not sacrifice your spontaneity and creativity. Picasso said: "It takes a long time to become young". Leave received ideas behind, do not be afraid to innovate, to be different. Be agile, opportunistic, obstinate and unafraid of mistakes and failures: embrace them, they shape us and bring us closer to success.

If the financial component is essential during the expansion of a business; according to you, money is less important than creativity at the beginning. You even go so far as to say: "Creativity can replace money."

Creativity is indeed decisive for success. If you make a watch that does not meet the expectations of the market, you will fail, no matter how much money you spend. The capital element is the idea; but an idea without a market cannot be successful. Creativity alone is not enough; Money alone is not enough. Money can only support a project that is in tune with a market need.

Mastering the art of provocation

You have a history of innovation, not only in watches themselves, but also in how to sell them. In 1984, for example, you succeeded in selling Blancpain watches at the Basel fair, without showing them (!), but by highlighting the specific values of the brand.

Wanting to be, as I said, "the first, different and unique", we decided NOT to show At the Basel fair, which is the great annual meeting of the profession! It was obviously very provocative: imagine a fashion show without models! Without clothes! We did not present watches, instead we highlighted our message: "Since 1735 there has never been a quartz Blancpain watch. And there never will be." We told our customers: "Before you look at the object, you have to understand what it wants to communicate to you. It is only when you know what Blancpain is, when you understand what is behind this name, that you can understand, appreciate and eventually want to acquire the one."

Understanding what the watch is, understanding the brand's philosophy and knowing its history make it possible to see the watch differently.

Exactly. That is the art of provocation. To provoke just for provocation's sake is sterile. There must be the substance behind the provocation. Our approach was certainly provocative but it had a profound meaning: to make people concentrate on what the object was.

How was your initiative perceived by the organizers of the fair?

We created an outcry: the fair's general management realized that if everyone did the same thing there would be only showcases without watches! So, we promised on our honour not to repeat this exercise, otherwise we would lose our stand. The following year, we presented JUST ONE SINGLE watch! *(Great laughter.)*

Another year, I hear you displayed a "FULL" sign in front of your booth?!

It is the same principle when selecting a restaurant: you choose the one where there are plenty of people. People attract people. To attract customers, you must say your restaurant is fully booked. The evening before the fair opened, we took the "FULL" sign from a restaurant and displayed it at the entrance of the Blancpain stand. Of course, once again it created an outcry: "Who do they think they are?!" Of course, thanks to the outcry, people were even more interested in us!

A more recent example of of innovation and even provocation is your association in 2017 with one of the most original TAG Heuer ambassadors: street artist Alec Monopoly, who started his career in New York.

Yes. Alec Monopoly – who as you know, always wears a top hat and keeps his face covered with a mask to remain anonymous (laughter) – became TAG Heuer's "Art Provocateur" after I asked him to tag our shop in Miami's Design District! My goal is clear: to continue to reconnect the brand to younger generations (the famous "millennials") with the help of Alec and others, and to explore new territories of expression, in marketing, distribution, communication. This sort of partnership helps to maintain TAG Heuer as an avant-garde brand.

Innovation all areas

You also innovate in the presentation of your watches, both commercially and technically. In the Hublot shop on Place Vendôme in Paris I saw a display with a mechanism that revealed the watch and then made it disappear.

If we want to show that we are at the forefront of innovation and technology, the way in which our watches are presented must also be at the forefront. It is a question of being coherent in all our actions. Thus, every year we innovate in window technology. Here again we are first, different and unique, because few of our competitors investing in R & D for showcases … Today the consumer wants an interactive showcase, a lively showcase and not just a static display case containing an inert product. We invested several million Swiss francs in research into the field of safe, glass-free showcases. The so-called Raptor makes it possible to present watches safely, since they disappear in the base at the rate of 2 metres per second as soon as anyone gets too close. We have the exclusivity on this patent for twenty years. They are very intriguing and spectacular showcases because they allow us to present watches worth millions of dollars without them being behind glass!

In Basel in 2012, you presented a Hublot watch inspired by the so- called "Antikythera Mechanism", a device invented in Greek antiquity. Here too, you innovate by reproducing the past, a very distant past!

It is a wonderful story. This "machine" was discovered by divers in 1900 in the wreck of a Roman ship off the island of Antikythera near Crete. It could have been designed and built by Archimedes about one hundred and ten years before the birth of Christ and is now considered to be the first astronomical calculator to indicate the movement of the Moon, the Sun and the stars. At the bottom of the wreck, in a corroded lump the size of shoebox, there were wheels, axes, gears creating a fabulous mechanism that was found to include three calendars: Metonic, Greek and Egyptian. The Antikythera Mechanism indicates the phases of the moon with a precision of seventy-two years, which means, after seventy-two years, there is just a one-day shift in relation to the actual position of the moon in the sky! In order to build this machine, it was necessary to know the rotation of the Moon to the second, the deviation corresponds to 0.15 seconds per day! The Antikythera Mechanism also indicates the eclipses of the Moon and the Sun and establishes the entire astronomical calendar of the then-known stars.

With the support and assistance of the Archaeological Museum of Athens and its curator Yanis Bitsakis who worked with us at the factory for three years on the project, we succeed in replicating the mechanism in a watch, within a diameter of 35 millimetres (the Antikythera machine measured 35 centimetres). Finally, we made three watches, which copied the functions of the Antikythera Mechanism to which we added two hands to indicate the hour and the minute. It was out of the question for us to sell these three watches, so we donated one to the National Archaeological Museum of Athens and another to the Hublot Museum. The third one was sold at auction by the Archaeological Museum of Athens to finance the continuation of studies on the Antikythera Mechanism. Although we could now produce these Antikythera watches and sell them, we refuse to do so because we believe that this treasure belongs to humanity and that commercialising such an important piece of mankind's cultural heritage is simply out of the question.

The Antikythera was the most complicated watch we have ever made. We would never have thought of building a watch featuring a moon phase indicator with a precision of 0.15 seconds per day. The Antikythera watch has taught us a lot. If someone had told me that we would learn from technology devised more than a century before the birth of Christ I would have replied that it was simply not possible.

In 2014, Hublot sponsored a new dive on the Antikythera site using a new advanced diving suit. Can you tell us more about an operation that was prepared in the greatest secrecy?

A second ship was identified near the wreck where the Antikythera Mechanism was found, Hublot decided to sponsor exploration of this new wreck using a unique SCUBA system called "Exosuit", developed by an American company. Apart from having exclusive images, Hublot was able to test its watch prototypes at great depths, under actual rather simulated conditions, which is, of course, a considerable asset.

4

"Tomorrow must be better than yesterday"

Realizing the impossible

From Tutankhamun to Magic Gold

Gérard Lelarge: At the same time as reviving a mechanism created more than one century before Christ, Hublot created a revolutionary new and decidedly 21st century alloy: Magic Gold, a precious metal that is scratch-proof. You presented this gold and ceramic alloy in 2011. What is the origin of this new material and what are its characteristics?

Jean-Claude Biver: In general, most high-end watches have been made of metals such as gold, platinum, steel and, in the late 20th century, titanium. We could add silver to that list, although this metal was not generally used for very high-end watches. Hublot has always been very active in metallurgical research and we had the idea to use our advanced alloy technology to try and remove the two main weaknesses of 18-carat gold: on the one hand its fragility (a gold watch that is not new always shows scratches) and its propensity to oxidize (18-karat yellow gold oxidizes over time).

We said, "If we can create a new 18-carat gold, we will have significantly advanced this precious metal" – every century needs to make improvements in all areas – and we will once again be first, different and unique. Tomorrow must be better than yesterday. The Swiss national anthem sings of it: the sun rises and presages a better day than yesterday, the exact words being:

'Sur nos monts, quand le soleil
Annonce un brillant réveil,
Et prédit d'un plus beau jour le retour.'

We mandated Professor Andreas Mortensen and his team in the mechanical metallurgy laboratory at EPFL; the Swiss Federal Institute of Technology Lausanne – one of the top ten research universities and research institutions in the world; to carry out basic research on a Scratchproof gold. We had to do more exploratory 'basic' research : rather than more focussed 'full' research, because the chances of success were extremely low and the risk of failure considerable

Finally, thanks to a gold and ceramic alloy, we succeeded in transforming 18-carat gold and giving it two unique and exclusive characteristics: a) it cannot be scratched (except by diamond, which is the hardest known material, and can scratch everything) and b) it does not oxidize. It is, therefore, a veritable revolution, the first great revolution in alloys since the time of Tutankhamun.

This 18-carat gold weighs less than 'traditional' 18 carat gold. It may be a stupid question, but does this mean that it is possible to make a watch with less gold?

No! That would be illegal! (Loud laughter.) There is no less gold! In one kilo of 18 carat gold, you have 750 grams of pure gold and 250 grams of alloy. Pure gold being 24 carats, the 18-carat gold is 18/24. This is why 18-karat gold is also called "gold 750". With Magic Gold, we always have minimum 750 grams of pure gold – otherwise we could not call it 18 carats – but the alloy is much lighter, so the whole is also much lighter. When we assay our gold, the gold content is higher than 750: it is 760, beyond the threshold.

To produce this new gold, Hublot has created a special foundry.

Indeed, we had to build a full metallurgical laboratory with, among other equipment, customized furnaces working under 2000 bars, that is to say the equivalent of a pressure of 20 000 meters under water, and to a temperature of 2200 degrees.

Search, again and again

Do you have patents for metals other than gold?

Yes, as the process can extend to silver and platinum, we have filed patents that protect us and give us exclusivity for twenty years. The process can also extend to aluminium (we know how to make scratch-resistant stainless aluminium!), but we could not file a patent on that since there were already very similar patents. We will soon be filing patents for other materials such as linen and red ceramic: development and creation must never stop.

Does this gold have a particular colour? Say "Hublot yellow" just as there is "Ferrari red"?

18-carat gold can appear in many colours: including red, pink, yellow, green. Since we already had yellow gold, pink gold and red gold in our collections, we chose to launch the first watch made using Magic Gold (the name given to our scratch-resistant, stainless 18 carat gold) in our Ferrari collection in green. Aesthetically it is what you might call a fairly technical colour. But of course we plan to make our Magic Gold in other colours and of course for other collections. We are also using other materials for which we own the patent, like for instance unscratchable platinum.

5

"A luxury watch tells more than the time"

Exceeding an object's functions

Understanding the function of a luxury product

Gerard Lelarge: For you "a luxury product indicates who you are". An haute horlogerie watch is an undeniable sign of success. You explain that "The watch is a communication tool."

Jean-Claude Biver: Today, a quality Swiss watch can communicate your taste, your sense of aesthetics, your social level, your personality, and so on. Because it is a communication tool, the watch gives information about who you are than it informs you of the exact time. It has a much greater value than if it had remained a mere timepiece. The watch has functions other than that of indicating the time. It has irrational functions: it can be a status-symbol, a vessel of emotion, a focus of our dreams. And today these are more important than the indication of the hour – the indication of time is commonplace: freely and universally available

This ticking instrument is nearly 400 years old and technically speaking it is obsolete because it is relatively inaccurate – as an indicator of the time, my phone is more accurate than my watch. On the other hand, a watch is remarkable as a piece of eternity. A quality mechanical movement can be repaired and maintained as long as there is a human being still able to handle tweezers and screwdrivers. A watch represents the love, passion and know-how of the men who made it. With a watch, you are dealing with a piece of cultural heritage, an art and a culture! Of course, machines help to make the components, but watches are made by men who invest them with their passion, their technical mastery, and their excellence and thus give birth to the soul of the watch. Your watch has a soul and to wear it is completely different to wearing a computer on your wrist

Conquering obsolescence

For you Japanese industry is handicapped by its failure to evolve the role of the watch, beyond its function as an indicator of the time.

Japan is a country with an enormous tradition, an extraordinarily refined culture, great subtlety and tremendous wealth. It is also very technologically advanced. Japanese industry is based largely on technology, and watchmaking has also followed this technological path. But when you make technology, you make obsolescence. The technology is made to be outdated; since every year new inventions appear. Unlike technology, art never becomes obsolete. A painting by Matisse or Renoir may not please the new generation but it cannot be obsolete. A Strauss waltz is not obsolete. The Japanese, for whom I have a profound respect and admiration, have not concentrated on watchmaking art, but on watchmaking technology: which is totally different.

Wait and understand … before you buy

You have defined a luxury product as "something that is recognised as a speciality for which you have to wait". Is a kind of "preparation", or initiation necessary to fully enjoy a luxury product?

True luxury always involves objects that have heritage, know-how, tradition, substance, and objective quality. Watchmaking art is heritage transmitted by a master craftsman. To understand the art and passion of the men and women who make watches, to understand the magic in their hands and the fingers; sensitivity and culture are necessary. To understand what Hublot is doing also needs preparation: as we know, Hublot not only repeats the past but adds elements of the future. It is this "fusion" that characterizes Hublot by marrying yesterday to tomorrow. Hence the advice I give: "Wait until you have understood our message before buying Hublot. First buy other watches. You'll be buying a Hublot later! I sometimes say of Hublot watches that "they are eccentric and different!" (Great burst of laughter.) These watches have an aesthetic that, is at first , unsettling. On the other hand, they appeal to those who have already bought other luxury watches and those who understand art.

Combining luxury – art – passion – love

It is said that "a luxury brand can make you dream about an exceptional universe and a myth". I imagine that you share this point of view.

Of course. That is why Hublot sponsors football and makes young people dream. If young people see Hublot from the age of 15 Hublot will be a myth and an icon for them by the time they are 30 years old. Louis Vuitton for example is an icon brand. With luxury, we are in the realm of the irrational, the world of dreams and art. Art is part dream, part emotion. But most of all art is love because it is governed by passion, which is a form of love. Hublot's watchmakers are passionate as are its managers.

Beyond the materials used and the time spent by exceptional artists and craftsmen, does a luxury product have to be expensive?

A luxury product is often expensive, because it is synonymous with excellence. It is therefore by definition more expensive than a mass-produced item. But beyond that, the luxury product makes it possible to acquire a small piece of legend, dream, heritage, culture and eternity.

Peter Drucker wrote: "It is the consumer who determines what the business is. What is important is what the consumer believes he is buying, it is his own conception of the value he attributes to the product." In your opinion, in terms of creation, who decides? The customer or the company?

Both. In the field of art – technology is different – the customer's requirement is difficult to apprehend. So we can do relatively little research on the market. We try to get to know our client and we try to make suggestions to meet a future need or to awaken new emotions. So, in the end, it is the client who decides: if he can not say precisely what he wants, he knows how to answer: "Yes, I like it." We must anticipate the expectations of the client. As Steve Jobs said, "A lot of times, people don't know what they want until you show it to them". He was right. And he quoted the line often ascribed to Henry Ford: "If I had asked people what they wanted, they would have said faster horses."

To go back to the field of luxury goods, I would like to reflect on an observation by Gaston Bachelard. He wrote in The Psychoanalysis of Fire: "The conquest of the superfluous gives a spiritual excitement greater than the conquest of the necessary." He added: "Man is a creation of desire and not of need." Do you share this analysis?

Yes. This is what makes the richness of the product of luxury. Luxury is superfluous. Even if at some point luxury is the return to simplicity.

6

"With watches I rediscovered the steam engine of my childhood"

Successful first steps

Learn to sell emotion

Gérard Lelarge: In 1975, you moved to the Joux Valley, the cradle of Swiss watchmaking. The choice of this place was symbolic of a desire to immerse yourself in the midst of tradition and excellence. You took your first steps at Audemars Piguet, where you were hired you immediately by the CEO Georges Golay. From that time you experienced, the great joy and great good fortune of learning the craft.

Jean-Claude Biver: Thanks to Frédéric Piguet, the father of my friend Jacques Piguet, I began my first job as a young graduate of the HEC business school. But for a whole year I was only paid a half salary, I had no office, no phone line, no secretary, no business cards, I took no business trips… Georges Golay, CEO of Audemars Piguet, told me that I did not need any of these things. He said: "First of all the job is to learn the trade in the workshops. You will watch, and you will listen to the watchmakers; through them and their way of life you shall learn the tradition and the art of watchmaking. "This is what I did, and over eight months I discovered the skill and passion of these men. This experience and especially my fascination with the art of watchmaking do not just enable me to sell watches, above all they enable me to talk the wonderful world of watchmaking and to inspire my clients before they sell a watch.

It has been proved that telling a story rather than just showing an object, stimulates a greater desire to buy. It is an essential principle that I continue to apply: to sell a brand, one must first learn to create emotions and make people dream. But today many products have more stories to tell and few companies still know how to create emotions and dreams.

It is logical that you were ambitious. As a young employee, you wanted to progress and make a career in the business. But your hopes were soon dashed.

Obviously I had ambitions, I was also certain that I could do some things differently, even better. My ambition is born of my will; when you are passionate and believe that you can do better, you want to implement your ideas to influence things. Alas! Georges Golay did not let me. He said, "Yes, you can do things differently but you will have to wait fourteen years." In other words when I was 43 years old! When you are 29 years old, you think that 43 is ancient. It was more impatience than ambition made me leave Audemars Piguet.

Hence the importance for companies to know how to "retain talent", and "ensure the loyalty of the best." Again, without anticipating what you will say us to your management style, what principles of management can you now highlight?

Again, my three commandments. The loyalty of men is ensured by sharing, respecting, and forgiving. First sharing: if you reject the ideas of valued employees, if you do not welcome them, if you do not share, one day they will look elsewhere. You have to share, welcome, adopt the ideas of employees and ask them to help you achieve them. Then respect: by consulting him, you respect your employee. Finally, forgiveness; be prepared to say, "it did not work this time but it does not matter, next time we will succeed."

Seize opportunities

In 1978, you were 29 years old, you left Audemars Piguet for Omega where you soon became director of the gold department

I joined Omega thanks to my brother Marc who ran the time-keeping section and worked directly with marketing director, Fritz Ammann, who became one of my best friends. Fritz Ammann said to Marc: "If your brother wants to come to Omega one day, we will welcome him with open arms." I accepted his offer right away and I became product manager for all Omega watches made of precious metal, gold or platinum. This was an incredible windfall. At 30, I became the youngest deputy director of Omega.

The late 1970s saw the birth of the quartz watch that changed the industry and gave the Japanese the opportunity to flood the market with cheap timepieces. For you the success of the quartz watch and decline of the Swiss watch were synonymous with the end of an era: that of the mechanical watch, dear to you since childhood.

I found it very difficult to be inspired by the quartz watch, even though everyone, even in Switzerland, thought this was the future. For me, the quartz watch is not a watch; it is quartz is made to resonate by a negative current on one side and a positive current on the other. Quartz vibrates millions of times per second (!) And a transformer converts these millions of vibrations million into a single vibration. This is why the second hand of a quartz watch moves every second, while the hands of a mechanical watch are constantly in motion. With Quartz watches, you have almost have no need for watchmakers any nimble hands will do. When I looked at a Quartz watch I no longer saw my steam engine; I had lost my toy. That's why in 1981, with my friend Jacques Piguet, I bought Blancpain; to revive the production of "real" watches, watches that tick, watches made by human hands.

In terms of innovations, in 1979 Omega launched the thinnest watch in the world (less than 2 millimetres thick); it was called the Dinosaur. What was the result of this project?

With Quartz watches, everyone had access to the same technology almost simultaneously; so it became very difficult to differentiate. To try to achieve this, brands were moving towards increasingly extreme miniaturization. This was the case of the Dinosaur project, an ultra-thin watch, launched in part to prove what Omega was capable of. But this watch did not have much commercial success; the name was turned out to be appropriate because like the dinosaurs this watch became extinct *(Big laugh)* It turned out to be a prediction!

But technically, the Dinosaur brought important innovations. It is a transparent watch: the mechanism is seen – as much as one can talk of a mechanism in a quartz watch *(sarcastic laugh)*! This innovation is fascinating because part of this technique would inspire the production of Swatch. Indeed, to save overall height, the caseback of the watch was also the baseplate of the movement. 1982 the Swatch applied the same principle that significantly reduced the number of parts and saved on labour thanks to simplified construction methods.

Search for the stroke of genius!

The early 1980s saw the restructuring of the Swiss watch industry and the appearance of the Swatch.

The difficulties of Omega were such that the banks and the Swiss Confederation decided to launch a restructuring plan for the watch industry. They entrusted this project to Nicolas Hayek who developed a plan advocating that a variety of businesses and brands be gathered under the same roof to better rationalize production costs. This 'roof', which sheltered numerous SMEs which were thus able to avoid closure, was called Société de micromécanique et d'horlogerie (SMH), which would later become the Swatch Group.

Thanks to Swatch (an abbreviation of Swiss Watch), Nicolas Hayek gave new impetus to Swiss watchmaking: producing a watch less expensively than the Japanese, and especially by creating a specific watch, a watch with a fashionable and slightly provocative image. Even today, wearing a Swatch, you do not have the feeling you are wearing a cheap watch, even if you bought it for 50 euros. With a 50 euro Swatch, you can go anywhere. The genius of Nicolas Hayek was to give an image of high quality and scarcity to a watch of this price; which had never been done before. Also on the retail level, while foreign watches were sold in tobacconists, displayed crammed together like sardines, the Swatch had a distribution was system selective, even exclusive. Nicolas Hayek was able to give this product a luxury image with a marketing policy identical to the one you would use for a luxury product.

7

"With Blancpain I could make a ticking watch"

Multiplying his investment by nearly 3000% in ten years

Gérard Lelarge: In 1981 Omega changed hands and you left the company, disappointed not to be able to relaunch the mechanical watch at a time when all your competitors selling quartz watches. You returned to the Joux Valley and began your adventure with Blancpain, a company created in 1735 that had stopped production before the introduction of quartz watches. Thanks to you, under the slogan "The oldest watch brand in the world" Blancpain soon became a great traditional luxury watch brand.

You bought the company with Jacques Piguet in 1981, for 22000 Swiss francs (about 20000 euros). Ten years later, you sold it for 60 million! How did you manage this feat?

Jean-Claude Biver: Simply by being the first, different and unique, but obviously also with our passion, our selflessness, our idealism, our naivety, sometimes our opportunism and of course our unlimited capacity for work. Also thanks to our faith, our stubbornness and thanks to the expertise of a team around us, who advised us and helped us achieve our goals. And finally, thanks to strict product quality. We always managed the business prudently and spent one when we had one and a half. So much so that in 1992 Blancpain had no bank debt, nor lease, nor mortgage, nor shareholder loans. Instead the company had 12 million Swiss francs in cash and was making an annual profit of ten million. It was employing a hundred watchmakers. So it was worth at least 60 million Swiss francs.

Dare to surprise

You simply bought the name "Blancpain".

Yes. In 1981, the company was just a name, moreover a name that had been absent from the market for yesrs, a forgotten name, and therefore at the time the Blancpain was not worth more than 22 000 Swiss francs. Jacques Piguet and I bought that name with a single purpose: not give birth to a technological instrument with quartz; but a TRUE watch – a ticking watch.

Your communication was simple: "Since 1735 there has never been a Blancpain quartz watch. And there never will be." This slogan was amusing since Blancpain had ceased its activity before the appearance of quartz watches!

Our message was clear: we have existed since 1735 and we are faithful to our art. This was why we said there will never be quartz watch; it is not a product of art, but technology. We produce watches that tick, that have mood swings, and that stop if we do not wind them; just like those of our grandparents. In other words watches that will not go out of style, watches with a soul, watches that are eternal! By contrast, quartz watches are doomed to obsolescence and one day can no longer be repaired.

Innovate in tradition

Blancpain was one of the first brands to return to mechanical watchmaking. Your innovation was to go against the grain, which gave you great visibility on the market.

Our return to the past was actually very innovative and of course it awakened curiosity immediately. People were surprised:

"1735!" The watch was completely classical; it had a beautiful pigskin strap, stitched by hand in a small workshop in Paris.

In terms of design, you also returned to a traditional aesthetic: the round shape. Why?

We were inspired by the drawings of children: when a child draws a watch, it is always round. Clocks in towers are round; as were the first watches of the 16th and 17th centuries. The circle is the most traditional expression of watchmaking.

Enduring by escaping trends

Blancpain became THE reference in watchmaking.

Blancpain was the standard of the tradition of watchmaking; and a standard never changes: it is immutable. So the shape of the watch should never change. *(JCB punctuated his words by hitting his pen on the table.)* The Blancpain watch had to be above fashion. The only way to continue is to escape trends. Therefore we chose to develop the Blancpain aesthetic through this classicism.

You wanted to stay faithful to the heart of the art of watchmaking, so you returned to traditional methods of work and the old ways of organization.

Yes, because everything had to be consistent. If I want to be consistent and strive for excellence, I cannot work in a factory: I have to work in a 'manufacture'. In a factory mass-produced parts are made by machine; in a manufacture, work is done by hand. If I want to be consistent, every watchmaker must make the watch from A to Z; he should be a "universal watchmaker" not a specialised watchmaker. The specialised worker was born with industry and only knows how to perform a part of the manufacturing process. With the traditional organization of labour, each worker knows everything and comes to work when he wants, including Sunday! This creates a lot of enthusiasm, because with this status comes responsibility; giving freedom is to give the responsibility. Each worker has the opportunity to be his own boss, and master of his work. This is essential.

Mastering the visible and invisible

Blancpain technical successes are well known. Tell us more about the production and manufacture of Blancpain's "six masterpieces of watchmaking art."

A masterpiece is a watchmaking complication that a watchmaker must make in order to be recognized as a master. This art includes six masterpieces: the ultra-slim; the moon phase (the watch reproduces on its dial the lunar cycle: new moon, first quarter, full moon, last quarter); the perpetual calendar (the date displayed on the watch is corrected automatically, leap year or not); the split-second chronograph (the watch has an additional second hand that 'splits' to measure intermediate times and then catches up with the other hand instantaneously); the tourbillon (a device that improves accuracy by counterbalancing disturbances of the balance wheel due to the gravity of the Earth) and finally the minute repeater (the watch strikes the hour, quarter hour and minutes).

Blancpain specialized exclusively in the manufacture of these six masterpieces, buying a Blancpain watch, you were sure to have an exceptional watch. It is worth remembering that the Blancpain minute repeater cost the equivalent of 150 000 euros at the time.

For Blancpain, you developed what you called "visible invisibility", a concept which would be revisited with the All Black Hublot. You say that "the strength of a watch lies in what it invisible." Can you explain your point of view?

It is essential to master the invisible, that is to say, the details that the customer does not see. Just because no one sees such a detail is no reason for not mastering it. On the contrary, it is because nobody sees it that it must be mastered. If by chance one day a watchmaker dismantles the mechanism, he will say "Wow! It is even polished here!" *(Cry of admiration.)*

In the early 1990s, you helped revive the manufacture of "erotic" watches.

These watches are an extremely complicated art. Watchmakers who made such watches created automata that reproduced scenes of nature and every-day life, inspired by paintings by Fragonard and erotica. Erotic watches cost a fortune. The erotic part of the watch is not seen immediately: you must lift a cover to discover the scene. Blancpain, published a book on erotic watches with Eric Othenin-Girard. The manufacture of these watches was discreet: we produced only three, four, or five per year. Technically they are very complex and require mastery of enamels: the scenes are enamelled in layers of colour, of a tenth of a millimetre. There were also very cheap erotic watches such as those sold in tobacconists. But that is another thing entirely…

Alongside a "great man"

In 1992 you sold Blancpain to Nicolas Hayek's SMH (later to become the Swatch Group). For you, it was best way to guarantee the continuity and tradition of Blancpain.

Certainly. At the time SMH was the number one watchmaking group in the world. It had extensive technological expertise but was hardly oriented towards luxury brands: the only luxury brand of the group then was Omega. Mr. Hayek wanted to go higher than Omega. To get on the luxury ladder, he decided to make acquisitions; first the purchase of Blancpain and then of Breguet, Jacquet Droz, Glashütte, etc. The sale of Blancpain was a *win-win:* it answered the wishes of SMH and Mr. Hayek, while giving us the security of being part of a group with perfect mastery of technology.

When you talk of Nicolas Hayek, you say "Mr. Hayek."
Yes, I did not call him "Nicolas", always "Mr. Hayek." Today I do not want to refer to him as just "Hayek". He was a great man.

What image do you have of him today?
That of a young man. Although the oldest in the group, he was often the most creative, and provocative. He had this incredible quality of mastering industry, business, marketing, trading and finance! He was gifted with great intelligence and finesse. He was always three steps ahead. He was a great visionary. In short, an exceptional man.

Transforming a torn cloth into a trampoline

You were in New York when the sale of Blancpain was concluded in July 1992 and when your assistant, Rose Christen, phoned to tell you, you burst into tears.

It was horrible! The sale of Blancpain was a time of the deepest depression a young entrepreneur can experience. Just to explain for a moment: an entrepreneur is always alone at the time of the decision. The loneliness of the entrepreneur is never talked about. Of course, he can have company on the journey; like I did he can make an appeal for consensus; but when the decision must be made, he alone is at the helm. At times this loneliness can cause stress and even a kind of depression.

In hindsight, I think Jacques Piguet and I were very alone at the time of sale; we had doubts. And Mr. Hayek was once again very smart: he realized that he had to act quickly because he understood that we did not quite know what we were doing!

(Laughter)

Blancpain was sold! I had to cancel meeting I had scheduled with Tiffany, take the plane and go home. At the time I felt it was a tragedy, a terrible wrench. But thanks to the sale, I was able to get to know Mr. Hayek and to spend twelve years working in the largest watchmaking group in the world. I was able improve some of my skills relaunching Omega and with what I learnt, I could then develop Hublot and finally sell it to LVMH, and have the privilege of working for the number one luxury group in the world, and to meet Mr. Bernard Arnault for whom I have enormous respect and by whom I am frequently inspired. So, the wrench of selling Blancpain eventually transformed into something positive. Although on the day of the sale I thought the world was falling apart.

For many years you regretted selling Blancpain.

Yes, for almost ten years. I did not see how I could ever do anything as exciting and as different as Blancpain because I thought it could never be repeated.

So you turned a page and that was for you the beginning of a new adventure, or rather a new success story, that of Hublot, a company created in 1980 by Carlo Crocco, who had represented the Blancpain brand in Italy. You bought a 20 % stake in Hublot, you joined the Board of Directors and soon became CEO.

8

"At Hublot, we marry yesterday to tomorrow"

So many big bangs – Merging the past and the future

Gérard Lelarge: After having left the Swatch group at the end of 2003, you wanted to make a comeback without betraying Blancpain. But why choose Hublot?

Jean-Claude Biver: Because from the beginning Hublot had fused materials that had never been associated: gold and natural rubber. It's like merging the past and the future. I made, remade, and mastered the past with Blancpain, so why not connect the past with the future? In doing so, I did not reproduce Blancpain, but created something different.

The distinctive porthole shaped watches, swiftly met with huge success worldwide. By using high-tech materials these watches have attracted the modernity-obsessed young people of the 21st century .

Hublot adds a new dimension to watches. It respects tradition – continuing to make watches that tick! But innovates with new materials and new colours. This innovation in tradition is seductive for the younger generation, which adopts these new materials quickly. The younger generation understands what Hublot is doing and influences the older generation, who may well be tempted to buy what young people are buying. What seduces the young attracts the old.

You call your communication 'disruptive', breaking with the traditional codes of luxury watchmaking.

Indeed, to the extent we marry extremes (tradition and the future, precious metals and materials such as carbon or rubber), our message is different. It enables us to attract very different customers to those traditionally targeted by luxury watchmaking: top athletes, rappers, and start-up designers who although millionaires only wear T-shirts, jeans… and also 200 000 euro watches!

For the creation of the new Hublot watches, you partnered with a renowned designer, Miodrag Mijatovic, known as Mijat in the world of watchmaking, with whom you have collaborated since 1982. Together you launched the concept of "fusion", combining futuristic materials with more conventional materials such as gold, platinum, and steel.

Indeed, Mijat, like other of my collaborators has accompanied me in my professional life since 1982. Others since 1979, and younger ones since 1996. I believe in teams that are welded by years of working together. I have always thought that my strength came from my teams. It is they who bring the success, and success should be dedicated to them. My collaborators take a share of success while I shoulder the setbacks. That is my idea of the role of a boss. He is there to motivate, train, transmit, team-build, and take responsibility for failures, while leaving success to his teams.

Hublot is not content to repeat the past, but adds elements of the future. Moreover, the concept of "fusion" is found in other areas such as: food, music and architecture. Today this trend is even evident in museums, which open their doors to let the future in by welcoming contemporary artists. Fusion is a general trend.

Destroy to rebuild

In 2005, you launched the Big Bang, a perfect expression of Hublot's "Art of Fusion". Linked to the creation of the world, the name 'Big Bang' name symbolizes your desire to bring out a totally new concept.

Our watch is called Big Bang for two reasons. First: it "deconstructs" a tradition to reconstruct a new one. That's exactly what the big bang did. Second: our watch blends rubber and gold, two materials that hitherto had never been associated with each other. Again, this fusion of elements very different to one another characterizes the Big Bang perfectly.

I often read that the Hublot watch is made like a sandwich… which, a priori, seems particularly surprising for a luxury watch. Can you be more precise ?

Yes, the Hublot watch was the first to inspire the term "sandwich" construction! Again, we were at the forefront. Usually watches are constructed like a pot: a classic watch is a box into which you put a mechanism that is covered with a transparent lid. With the watch-sandwich we can stack several components one on top of the other and play with various combinations of materials and colours.

The success of the Big Bang was immediate. In its first year, the watch received the Design Award at the Geneva Watchmaking Grand Prix. Numerous international awards over the following years helped accelerate the revival of Hublot.

Yes, because at that time the watch was very innovative in both its design and its content. We won all the awards and prizes possible.

Innovation in materials

How far do you think you can go with the "fusion" of materials very different from each other?

The possibilities of fusion are endless. As and when new materials are invented, we follow them closely: Hublot's intention is to be the first to use new materials … which traditional brands will use in ten or twenty years. But the material used must have assets compared to its predecessor. For example, ceramic has four advantages: it is scratch resistant, hypoallergenic (for example is used to manufacture artificial hips), colourfast, and is 30 % lighter than steel.

Hublot continues to innovate; you even created a bracelet that is a "fusion" of alligator and rubber!

In order to achieve the effective fusion of materials, we combined crocodile skin – which is not very water-resistant – and rubber. The rubber on the skin is always dry and the strap, whether pigskin, ostrich or crocodile can dry in the sun.

The Mag Bang was created in 2006 in a numbered series of 250 pieces. The press spoke of it as a UFO. Why was that ?

With this watch we embraced the 'ultra-light' trend. New materials, such as plastics and magnesium, have contributed to the progress of F1, boats, aircraft (I am thinking of the A380), computers … Hence our idea of making watches in lightweight materials. Thus the mechanical movement – the HUB44 exclusive to Hublot – and the housing of the Mag Bang are made of magnesium, the lightest metal in the world. For the first time a watch was brought to market that cost more than if it had been made of precious metal!

In 2013, Hublot made a bright red ceramic watch thanks to a new manufacturing process.

Again, it was a major technical first for red ceramic to have the same qualities as black ceramic and white ceramic. This watch (the Red 'n' Black Skeleton Tourbillon) paid tribute to the colours of the Principality of Monaco for the 5th Only Watch auction held in 2013, to support research into Duchenne muscular dystrophy, a disease that affects 250 000 people worldwide. Hublot created this unique watch, as part of this fundraising event organized under the patronage of Prince Albert II of Monaco.

Another innovation in material: the partnership with Berluti concluded in 2016.

Not only the strap, but also the face of the Hublot Classic Fusion is made from Venezia leather, the patinated leather emblematic of the brand. This watch is used the same procedures as those used for leather shoes at Berluti: cutting, shaping, and lacquering are identical.

Innovation in design

You created watches of larger diameter: 41, 44 and even 48 millimeters. How does this case, which may seem oversized, adapt to small wrists?

The largest possible diameter of a watch is that of the wrist. We never develop a new watch without addressing the need for client comfort; he must be able to wear his watch without thinking about it, regardless of its size. But this notion of comfort is sometimes forgotten by some brands that produce watches that meet their technical requirements, such as size and thickness of the movement, without thinking about customer convenience and expectations.

You make me think of a slogan of Carlos Ghosn, then head of Nissan, "stop making cars for engineers," they may be technically perfect, but do not meet customer requirements.

This is actually a common mistake particularly encountered in watchmaking. How do you design a product that is in line with the expectations of your customers? Including the customers of tomorrow; whence our partnerships with the world of football and the design of a watch for the rapper Jay-Z. Luxury brands must learn to speak to the new generation, even if it is not yet able afford to buy expensive watches. This why Hublot and TAG Heuer have partnerships in football, and TAG Heuer in cycling, a sport to which the brand has returned after twenty years of absence.

Another innovation: creating a black model on black (the All Black), when until now black watches were often low end.

Exactly. Most Black watches undergo a specific treatment – the so-called *physical vapor deposition* (PVD) – to blacken the case, but these watches are easily scratched and the material underneath is not really black. Our All Black is totally different: it is composed partly of ceramic, so it is scratch proof and unalterable. Even if you expose it to ultraviolet light for a thousand years, the black ceramic will remain black. Another feature is that everything is black: the watch, the dial, hands and indexes! So in principle invisible! This is our challenge: even from a metre you see only black. But as the hands are polished and the rest of the watch is matte, the hands can be identified by the play of of light on the matte and polished surfaces. Again, we were a leader: some watch companies have followed suit and black has become a high end trend.

In 2014 you created a collection of watches available only in Hublot boutiques worldwide.

This is the *Limited Edition – Hublot Boutique Exclusive* collection, of which a special series is created each year. The first was the Big Bang Unico All Black, whose ambassador is Usain Bolt. The fusion of matte black with blue, red, green and orange enabled the roll out of this model.

In terms of design, you always continue to innovate: for instance in 2013, there were "jeans" watches sold between 15 000 and 18 000 euros. What was the innovation here?

It came from an idea of Tina Zegg in Monaco (the retailer representing the Hublot brand in the Principality), Hublot created a watch with a dial and bracelet made with the same Italian distressed denim that the manufacturer supplies to all the big names in luxury and fashion. In 2016 Hublot continued to innovate and presented the "jeans" watch in a more intense black and introduced ceramic. That was the birth of the Big Bang Ceramic All Black Jeans. Two versions were created, limited to one hundred pieces each. The male version has a diameter of 44 mm, the female version is available in 41 mm and is set with 36 black diamonds. The dials and straps are made fromblack denim, but without the "distressed" look of the first model.

Also in 2013 creating fluorescent watches.

For the Big Bang Fluo, which plays on the contrasts between black and eye-catching colours, four versions are available: blue, yellow, pink and green, each limited to 250 numbered copies.

Innovation in Technology

Among recent creations is the Oceanographic 4000, water-resistant to a depth of 4000 meters, endorsed by the Oceanographic Museum of Monaco and the Albert I^st^ Prince of Monaco Foundation.

This is to show our expertise and mastery of technology. Again Hublot achieved a world first by manufacturing the first commercially available watch to descend to such depths.

Models making collections such as Big Bang, King Power, Classic Fusion or Masterpiece house particularly complex watch movements such as tourbillon, minute repeater, split-second, foudroyante, retrograde date, etc. One imagines that the complexity of these mechanisms characterises the unique character of a luxury product.

The luxury watch is characterized by the objective quality of the work and, as already noted, by the amount of "invisibility" mastered, that is to say finishing, in places the customer do not see. The luxury watch is also distinguished by the complexity and the difficulty of making the movement, the more difficult a movement is to make, the more you are certain to be different, or even unique.

For its "complicated watches," Hublot has created a special collection, collection MP, for MasterPiece. Which watches make up this collection?

They are watches with unusual movements that are the result of the latest research in the fields of mechanics and engineering. The first piece of the collection was the MP-01, created in 2011 and only 100 were made. This is a tonneau (barrel)-shaped watch in titanium, with a ten-day power reserve thanks to its three barrels working in series. The second piece in the collection is the Key of Time, the first watch with the time of "your" choosing at the speed you like it. Thanks to a three-position crown, this watch can change as desired the speed at which the hours and minutes pass. You can make the pleasant moments last four times longer… and reduce the length of all the painful moments… while obviously having the ability at any time to return to "real time"! Only 50 examples of this watch were made.

Two other innovations in the technical field: first a system that allows you to be informed in real time, thanks to an alert on your mobile phone, when a Hublot is sold anywhere in the world. And also, the creation of a smart card – called Hublotista – provided at the time of purchase. What is its function ?

Once inserted into a reader, that smart card authenticates the watch and accesses a website exclusively for owners of Hublot, who can benefit from various privileges such as being invited to parties or special events.

Innovating in the industrial process

In terms of industrial processes, Hublot can now manufacture its watches from A to Z, including alloys made in its own workshops. Why this strategy?

This is of course to secure our supplies and our production, in order to be able to innovate as we please, without being dependent on a third party. But having a proprietary movement is not just a matter of technical independence; it is also a matter of creative independence, and authenticity that gives the brand credibility and contributes to its overall image.

In 2009 a new high-tech factory was inaugurated in Nyon on the shores of Lake Geneva allowing the size of the factory to double by 2015.

In fact this factory, where older machines only 'date back' to 2008 and where workshops are close to those of F1, allow us to perform new tasks and ensure the independence of almost all of our production. In the same spirit – in order to reduce its dependence in the supply of movements and springs – TAG Heuer has invested in its own factories creating a plant in Chevenez, Switzerland, near the French border in 2013.

Innovation in pricing

In 2007 a million-dollar watch made its debut. A few words about the highly original genesis of this watch?

The million-euro watch came out of a drawing and a phone call in my car. One of my gem-setter friends suggested creating a watch that would be a world first (always first, different and unique) made entirely with invisible setting. The invisible setting – in which a precious stone is set in a recessed frame to create an uninterrupted surface of gemstones – was developed by a Place Vendome jeweller early last century. It was often used to make brooches shaped like flowers, butterflies, dragonflies, etc., but never for a watch. Thanks to precision within a tolerance of two or three microns, we could, said my friend, do the same invisible setting for a watch. I give him my agreement and I immediately telephoned to Tina Zegg, our client in Monaco, to whom I explained, "I'll make a unique watch, a world first, a watch at $1 million, I'll sell it to you." She replied: "That's serious money; give me fifteen minutes and I will call you back." Fifteen minutes later, she called me back, and she bought the watch. In a quarter of an hour, I had ordered and sold the watch. All this on the phone. No paper. This is the old way of working among watchmakers, diamond dealers, and bankers: a verbal order is as good as written one. It's beautiful when your word is enough to do business and you can manage without a sixty page contract.

A two million dollar Hublot was presented at the Monaco Grand Prix in 2011. The following year, you unveiled a five million dollar watch at the fair in Basel.

The price of these watches depends on the number of carats. It is the addition of jewelry, stone cutting and setting is an extraordinarily difficult task at this level, which is we achieve these prices. It is logical that we made watches with diamonds; watches and jewelry are long associated; they are neighbouring trades. While in 1540 there were more than 600 artisan jewellers in Geneva but not a single watchmaker. Then the Huguenots brought watchmaking. So, in 1601 when the guild of master watchmakers was created, there were more than 600 watchmakers: suddenly, there were as many watchmakers as jewellers.

What are the features of the 5 million dollar watch?

It is a white gold watch decorated with 1282 diamonds of perfectly consistent quality and colour. In total, more than 140 carats of diamonds, from all over the world, were mounted. Six of these diamonds weighed more than 3 carats each. The manufacture of this watch required fourteen months of full time work and involved 12 cutters and five setters. It was sold to a retailer in Singapore.

What you will make after this 5 million dollar watch?

Exceeding that price would require a larger number of diamonds; which I think is difficult because the surface of the watch is limited (the 5 million-dollar Hublot has a diameter of 44 millimeters). We must do something exceptional to follow this watch. For example, why not replace glass of the dial with a sheet of diamond? That is one direction in which we can think.

Releasing Synergies

In 2008, LVMH bought Hublot. With this acquisition, Bernard Arnault strengthened his watchmaking division. What do you think led to LVMH to choose Hublot?

I think that choice is related to the fact that Hublot was already then a "rising star". Hublot was – and still is – a very dynamic company, growing strongly, totally different from others thanks to its DNA; a company that talks a lot to a young clientele; a healthy profitable company, which is totally self-funded and has no debts or mortgages; a company with a sharp concept and product. It should be noted that in 2004 the turnover of Hublot was 26 million Swiss francs and that in 2018 it stands at it will be above half a Billion. Every year it records strong growth.

The arrival of LVMH was probably preferable to the entry of a speculative investor; what benefits has Hublot derived from the arrival of Bernard Arnault?

The arrival of LVMH was actually preferable to other solutions. LVMH, the largest luxury group in the world, brings experience and synergies that are enormous. For example, cognac and watches have nothing in common, but there are synergies, particularly in China where Hennessy has a dominant position, with bottles that can sometimes sell 10 000 or 20 000 euros. Customers of Hennessy and Hublot may be the same, and we can work together on promotional activities. There are also examples of synergies with leather goods. Plus there are opportunities for economies of scale: when you buy advertising space in the media, the power of a group like LVMH gives you enormous advantages in terms of brand presence. LVMH also brings its expertise in *retail:* no luxury group in the world has as many stores as LVMH. I do not see any other group with which Hublot could generate more synergies. Of all the choices, I would say that LVMH was the best choice … apart from me!

Indeed, given the selling price to LVMH (490 million euros is the rumoured figure) you were not able to buy Hublot yourself. How did you view this situation?

I have nothing to complain about. First, because I›m still here, still enjoying myself, and still motivated. Moreover, as I had 20 % of the company, I was not exactly impoverished by the sale. I think things went well although I had a few weeks of regrets. At worst, I cry with one eye and laugh with the other.

Bernard Arnault has given you a large degree of autonomy within the LVMH group.

Leaving individual companies with plenty of independence is one of the group's policies. LVMH is a group that cultivates the entrepreneurial spirit, which means allowing people to take action. On the contrary, when you give too much guidance you kill the entrepreneurial spirit and create a "framework" instead of creating "entrepreneurs".

On 1st March 2014, you become president of watchmaking division of LVMH, which includes: Hublot, TAG Heuer and Zenith, the core around which orbit such jewellers as Chaumet, Fred, Bulgari and De Beers. What are the characteristics of the three brands and what are your main objectives?

The three brands have very complementary positionings: TAG Heuer represents "affordable luxury" with watches at an average price of around 3000 euros; Zenith is "high end traditional watchmaking" (8500 euros); and Hublot, a luxury and prestige brand, offers "ultra-high watchmaking" (18 500 euros and up). TAG Heuer has always been avant-garde; Zenith – a brand created in 1865 – symbolizes watchmaking tradition of which the famous El Primero movement, created in 1969 is the single most important element; and Hublot is, we know, the "fusion of tradition and the future."

You fulfil more functions today: you are president of the watch division of LVMH, Chairman of Hublot, CEO of TAG Heuer and – more recently – Zenith. What is your strategy?

Without revealing anything in detail, I have three objectives: to grow; to gain market share; and to create and manage synergies between the three brands while respecting their discrete DNA, positioning and philosophy. Beyond that, my goal is, if possible to "expand the family" today there are three children, but one day there may be four or five.

Preserving DNA at all costs

Hublot projects include China, where the market share is much lower than that of your competitors.

Hublot market share in Greater China (China, Hong Kong and Taiwan) is now only 20 % (against 30 % and more ACROSS the Swiss watch industry) because we started to develop the brand there are only in 2011. But in China the return on investment comes after eight or ten years. Today the Chinese still do not quite equate the sports watch with a luxury item (as was also the case in Europe in the 1950s).

I am often asked why I do not adapt myself to the Chinese market. Simply because I have only one DNA. I'm on stand-by: waiting until the Chinese are ready. If I changed my DNA today, tomorrow I might no longer be recognized by the Chinese who continue their Westernization. While it is true that we have designed a watch made only for Chinese (the dial is jade colour), we must be careful not to respond systematically to their demands because if we do that, the day the Chinese will have evolved, we will no longer be on their wavelength when they are ready for us.

What of LVMH's watchmaking division's plans for expansion abroad?

The group will develop in emerging territories, such as Indonesia, India (Zenith was the watch of Mahatma Gandhi), and South America. Hublot is very interested in the former Soviet republics, such as Kazakhstan, Azerbaijan, and Georgia. But China remains the priority. The country has shown phenomenal development potential in the mid-range: it is estimated that in a few years, the Chinese middle class will number between 500 and 600 million people.

You continue to develop your commercial network worldwide. What were the latest Hublot outposts?

After New York (Madison Avenue and Fifth Avenue); Atlanta Miami, Los Angeles, Dallas and San Francisco. In 2014 we created the "Hublot Gallery" in Miami›s Design District, an area that is home to many art galleries, and high-end luxury, and pret-a-porter boutiques. We opened our first store in Bangkok and eight stores in China in eight cities, including a second store in Shanghai in 2015. A store in Kuwait, brought the number of Hublot boutiques in the Middle East to seven. In Paris, we have had a Rue Saint-Honoré store since 2007 and another in Place Vendôme since 2011. Moreover, we have a shop in London. In total, we are currently available in over 800 stores worldwide, including nearly 80 monobrand stores always in very prestigious addresses, including La Croisette in Cannes and Fifth Avenue in New York in April 2016.

You communicate in China especially through sports partnerships such as Ferrari and Manchester United.

In China, we organize the same events and we proceed in the same way as in Miami, Paris or Zurich. And through the purchases that the Chinese make abroad, I feel that we are making progress. When a Western brand starts, the first purchases are rarely made in China because customers are wary at the beginning of Chinese retailers fearing that the models will not be the latest and the quality the same as elsewhere. They start buying in shops in France, Japan, Korea, Hong Kong, Switzerland… But not in China.

Give, do not just take

In the field of philanthropy, Hublot has developed various programmes benefitting the poorest, including the Hand in Hand Foundation, created about fifteen years ago by the company founder, Carlo Crocco. Hublot also supports the Smiling Children Foundation which aims to develop the education of girls in Morocco and Afghanistan.

Yes. Hand in hand Foundation is managed by Mr. Crocco; it takes care of orphanages in India and Hublot has supported it financially. It is the same for Smiling Children, where Cherie Blair is the patron.

Still on the charity work of Hublot, we can also include football and your action against racism.

During the Euro 2008, we advertised the theme *"No to Racism"*. Instead of a three metre long advertising banner on the corner line saying "Hublot"; we unfurled a banner against racism. We help the Foundation "Fight Against Racism". As a sponsor, I feel a responsibility: to give and not just take. Sponsors generally take but do not give. As a sponsor, we help the sport, that is a great educational tool.

What other philanthropic actions have you taken recently?

In 2013, with Falcao, the Colombian soccer star, we launched a large operation to fund work in the great swamp of Santa Marta with the United Nations Office against Drugs and Crime (UNODC). This funding was made by selling the watch Classic Fusion Falcao – a limited edition of only 100 pieces (60 in titanium and 40 in gold). Also in 2013, we partnered with Depeche Mode to benefit Charity Water, an organization that aims to provide clean water to developing countries. This is our second partnership with Depeche Mode since 2010, when we raised funds for the Teenage Cancer Trust, with a charity concert at the Royal Albert Hall in London.

9

"I love the adrenaline of victory. I am guerrilla at heart."

Succeeding as an outsider

Investing the maximum of self

Gérard Lelarge: You say that among the keys to entrepreneurial success are a colossal working capacity, strong creativity, a good emotional balance, determination and ambition and finally a great ability to bounce back.

First, to use your words, "a huge work capacity." "I never stop," you say. How do you manage to reconcile a particularly busy pace of work with family life to which you are very attached? In a video, we see you take a note out of your suitcase from your wife Sandra, it says: "Come back soon!"

Jean-Claude Biver: It is relatively easy: you have to work when the family is absent, that is to say at night. If you go to bed at 10 pm, young kids are in bed and if you wake up at 3 am, you will not miss the children as they are still asleep. From 3:00 to 7:00, you can work four hours without a guilty conscience since you are not separated from the family and the family is not separated from you.

You explain that work early in the morning allows you to be fully available when you're at your desk in the company.

Indeed: doing my *homework* from three or four in the morning helps me when I'm at the factory in Nyon, at 8:00 to 8:30, to be totally available for everyone: clients, journalists, visitors, suppliers and of course all my colleagues. When I get to my office, I have nothing to do since I did everything at home!

To invest so much of yourself so intensively you must have an amazing constitution. Do you ever get tired like everyone else?

I have the privilege of having an iron constitution even if, of course, I am sometimes tired; but like all who are passionate about what they do, I start again. Passion has no limits and overcomes fatigue. The cyclist arrives "exhausted" at the top of the Tourmalet but his passion is such that he is in the saddle again the next day. The climber who reached the summit of Everest says "never again"; but six months later, when he has treated his frostbite, he returns.

You do not spare your efforts. Legend has it that many years ago at the Basel fair, you slept in a Volkswagen camper van and in the morning you went to shower and shave at the railway station. Is this true?

That's right. Jacques Piguet did the same. After buying Blancpain, we had little money left. So, when we went to visit customers, we slept in a camper-van and not at an hotel, we went to shave and shower in stations, we put in a token and were entitled to three minutes of water. You had to shower fast!

Conquer, don't just manage

In addition to intense work, great creativity is also essential to the success of the entrepreneur. In this way you revived Blancpain and relaunched Hublot. You seem to prefer to conquer and relaunch rather than quietly manage.

Quiet management does not really tempt me! I like the adrenaline of conquest, the adrenaline of the risk and of innovation. I love to capture a position, to ambush, and conduct guerrilla warfare. I am a manager who gets his hands dirty rather than a corporate manager who directs. When the plane is at cruising altitude at 10 000 meters, and we are about to cross the Atlantic for six hours, I tend go on to autopilot!

You mention the term "guerrilla". For you, must an entrepreneur be a "guerrilla"?

Exactly. I'm guerrilla at heart. I try to surprise my competitors and my clients. We must take advantage of opportunities. This is the example of the little mouse riding on the back of the elephant that says, "How tall I am! How fast I am going!

Overcoming start-up handicaps

The lack of resources you had at your disposal when you began in the watch indstruy forced you to be particularly innovative. You say: "I have done things one needs to do when one is unknown and an outsider." Is this guerrilla behaviour?

That's right. Without means you must find shortcuts. Imagine that we are in a race to get to Paris. If I have a less powerful car that is slower than yours, and if I leave ten minutes after you, I will never catch up if I take the same road as you. However, if I take a different route, I might be there before you arrive. When one has no means and is the smallest, one must do things differently, and find other ways. This is what I call guerrilla behaviour. But one point is critical: always respect ethics and never act at the expense of honesty. I have got to Paris before by taking a different route, but I must not run down pedestrians! *Be opportunistic to seize an opportunity?* Yes. *Be opportunistic and disregard ethics?* No. Never.

I have read that in watchmaking you are the equivalent of Karl Lagerfeld in fashion: as much because of your creativity, as your conviction and your results. You have been personally honoured on numerous occasions, as CEO or manager of this or that year. Sometimes awards are given for "lifetime achievement"; others describe you as a "visionary businessman" and "marketing genius". Did you imagine this kind of consecration when you started in the luxury watchmaking?

Not at all. In my wildest dreams, I imagined having a maximum of 5 % of what I have today. So I received twenty times more than my wildest dreams. And not only as regards prizes and awards: all of my life has been twenty times better than I could have wished. I'm satisfied. If I had the right to live twice, I would not exercise this right unless I could be assured 100 % that I would live the exact same life. I give thanks every day, but I know that at any time what I have can be taken away: nothing is set in stone.

Have the courage to be wrong and use failure to bounce back

Succeeding as an entrepreneur also means enjoying emotional balance, particularly at the family level. The family is an indispensable foundation for your balance.

I need harmony and peace. Peace is given by me emotional balance. I cannot be creative unless I am in full possession of this peace and this inner harmony. Without love, no peace and with out peace, no performance.

Succeeding as an entrepreneur also means determination and ambition. With determination obstacles can be overcome. What are the difficulties faced by an entrepreneur and how can he emerge victorious?

I think the biggest challenge is to have, at some point, the courage to enact your vision. Many entrepreneurs have vision but they are slow or they do not dare to implement it for fear of being wrong. But you have to know that nothing is ever completely lost: to make a mistake is never the end. Business life is made of successes and failures, and one must be able to bounce back.

Beyond the family circle, what are the other sources of stability in your life?

There are always two energies: a negative and a positive. Life is always the *yin* and *yang*, day and night, hot and cold, water and earth. There is always an equilibrium to be found. If the pilot of diving aircraft operates the joystick properly, it will pick up speed and avoid the mountainside in its path. With martial arts, you take the energy of the aggressor and use it to overcome him. It is always important to find positive energy in negativity and failure.

In 1997, you contracted an illness first identified as double pneumonia, and treated as such, for three years, with little effect. In 2000, Professor Philippe Leuenberger, specialist in pulmonology, discovered the exact nature of the illness: Legionellosis. You were then immobilized at home for several months. How could a man as active as you survive this long hiatus?

Legionellosis was nature's early warning for me and in that sense it was extremely beneficial. It is no exaggeration to say that it was a real stroke of luck: illness allowed me to step back and showed me the need to think of myself more. We must lose health to realize its importance.

Professor Philippe Leuenberger advised you to leave the lake and settle in the mountains. So you bought the farm at Tour-de-Peilz where you live. The farm, which was a long-chereished dream has become a place of healing.

Always behave like a winner

Setting ambitious goals is critical to success. You put it this way: "To become stronger, think as if you were already strong."

One who is weak and acts as a weakling remains weak. One who is weak behaves as if he were strong at least gives himself a chance to become stronger. It's obvious. You cannot become strong if you have a defeatist attitude and if you behave like a weakling.

Onassis explained: "It is better to stay in a maid's room in a palace hotel rather than take a beautiful room in a one star hotel." Because when you are in the lobby of the palace, you might meet people who can help you and nobody knows that you're staying in the maid's room. But when you are at a one star hotel, you are unlikely to meet anyone! *(Big laugh.)* Therefore, it is imperative to act strong from the start.

Back in the Blancpain days, I took a stand-by ticket to New York; I was lucky to only wait one day (I was sleeping at the airport, in a sleeping bag) and have a cheap ticket. When I arrived in New York, I immediately phoned Tiffany. I told him: "I'd like to meet you tomorrow; I am currently in Switzerland, but I will take the Concorde to come to see you."

"You will not take the Concorde just to see me!"

"Yes, for you, I'll take the Concorde. Do you have lunch at noon?"

He said: "Yes, but only for half an hour."

"So, I will come for half an hour and have a sandwich with you. If after half an hour you realize that I have nothing interesting to say, you will not regret this half hour since in any case you take it for lunch. But if after half an hour you have learned something, well, you have eaten and in addition you will not have wasted your time."

The next day I was in New York…

10

"I am my intuition"

Simultaneously iconoclastic and efficient

Build strong personal relationships

Gérard Lelarge: Managing a business involves building strong personal relationships to motivate and mobilize. I imagine that you manage your teams that way.

Jean-Claude Biver: I manage my teams through sharing. When you share your knowledge, you enrich the team. When you share your doubts, rest assured the team that says, "Well, what do you know, he also has doubts." When you share your failures, you enrich the team, which learns from your mistakes and says: "Well, what do you know, he too makes mistakes." When you share your success, when you forgive the mistakes of your employees, you have a team that wants to help you. We want to help those who are sincere, respectful, sharing, forgiving, ethical. This way, you strengthen your management, like the swallow reinforces its nest. The swallow may fly away for a year, but when it returns, the nest is still there.

You explain that your office is always open. Why?

Apart from the main door, there are two more doors to my office! But none is ever closed. My office is not that of a boss, where I work alone, like someone important. I do not work in my office because, as you know, I work at home early in the morning. At the office, I listen, I encourage, I exchange, I share, I negotiate, I convince, I communicate, I suggest, I motivate, I assure, I forgive. It is a place where you can discuss and share ideas. My office is actually an *open space;* but it is also an *open heart,* an *open mind,* and *open eyes*. If I received a colleague behind closed doors, others would ask, quite logically, what is happening behind their back and perhaps to their detriment. That's why when I have to talk one-on-one, I go to a restaurant.

In the days of Blancpain, you would explain the traditions of watchmaking during your visits to retailers: you valued the salesmen and you created strong personal ties with them.

Some people walk straight past and barely say hello to salesmen. But who does the work every day? The owner of the jeweller on Place Vendôme or the sales staff? The first thing you must do is respect the work of the sales team.

Most major decision makers can judge their interlocutor in a few seconds. I imagine that you are one of them. Hence two questions: What are your criteria for judgment and you are you ever wrong?

Yes, sometimes I am mistaken, three or four times out of ten. Because I'm too naive; more precisely because I want to be naive. I want to give people the benefit of the doubt, and do not want to see the negative. I tend to trust at the beginning; and then only later do I tend to say no. When I'm wrong, it is because that I did not listen to my doubts.

What are your criteria for recruitment?

My criteria are simple: to some extent I have no professional criteria and I do not decide based on a CV and diplomas. I judge most of the time with my instincts and my intuition. I also attach great importance to the errors that the candidate admits to having made: when they are missing from the resume, I ask for at least two or three. Surprisingly, some are unable to remember having made any mistakes! This procedure is not Cartesian, but it works! Hence the importance of dialogue and lunch together. It is true that this is possible only with a small team: with 400 people, you can sense and know everything. If we were 80 000, it would of course be different: one would use other criteria.

It is also said that a leader is someone who has the courage to displease. Do you share this view?

Of course, the courage to say no and risk displeasure is very important. That is why entrepreneurs are bad politicians: we cannot make too many compromises and too many promises. You have to be rational and too bad if you do not like it. We need to voice truths: it is part of the responsibility of a leader.

Knowing with whom to surround yourself and to whom to listen

You rely on a loyal team. Mijat, designer at Hublot, worked with you in the revival of Blancpain. Ricardo Guadalupe successor to the head of Hublot in early 2012 is a longtime friend. One of your assistants, Rose Christen, has worked alongside you for many years. Your other assistant, Kari Palaz, has been working with you since 1979. Has your goal, throughout your career, been the building of a team of Biver's boys and Biver's girls?

In some cases I have worked with the same team since 1979. The team is the foundation of your success. A house is better if its foundations are solid. You can build on this. Without a team, you›re nobody. We cannot succeed alone. You take a winning team, you put it in Blancpain, it wins; you put it in Omega, it wins; you put it in Hublot, it wins. It's not the colour of the football shirt which wins the World Cup, it is the men who wear it. Surround yourself with people more competent than you are. You must be the conductor but you cannot be both the best guitarist and best pianist.

You know with whom to surround yourself, but do you listen?

I always look for consensus and I do not impose my ideas. As you know, the doors of my office and my conference room are wide open. Nobody should knock on my door because when you knock on a door, there is a barrier and I do not want that. I listen to everyone and everyone listens to me. We communicate in the elevator, in the kitchen, in the hall and not just in meetings. One of the privileges of being a small business is being able to ignore the mania for meetings in which everyone speaks but says nothing.

You handwrite many dozens of guarantees and letters a week.

Writing by hand is a sign of respect. Receiving an e-mail or SMS does not have the same effect as receiving a handwritten letter. If I have a great respect for you, I will pick up my pen to write to you.

When you sent me a handwritten letter during our first meetings and I was very touched.

Well, I'm glad I did. It is very rare that I respond with a letter that my secretary types. Most of the letters that I send are written by hand. Even so, I write a lot of emails, about 300 per day.

Dare to decide

The effective manager needs to decide. When you making a strategic decision how much is instinct and how much is rational?

There are no rules: there are some decisions that require more instinct and others that need to be taken much more rationally. For example, sponsorship is an area where many business leaders have gone astray: their financial commitment has often been proportional to their own pleasure. You need to adapt to what the decision requires.

Even if speed of decision is an important factor in success, one cannot ignore the importance of being able to step back and pause for thought.

A decision made quickly can be excellent and the same decision taken too late may no longer be appropriate. Speed is an extraordinary ally; if your timing is wrong the decision will be bad. But if you decide quickly, you must be able to make adjustments. However, if you cannot change things quickly if you make a mistake, it is imperative to take time to come to a decision. The general rule is to try both to decide quickly and, if necessary, have the flexibility to make changes quickly.

Still on the subject of decision-making, do you decide you primarily based on past experience – lessons learned – or rather on as much of the future as far as you can predict it?

Evidently the past is important: it allows you to project. The past is a diving board. You cannot make a beautiful dive, standing at the poolside. You need the flexibility of the diving board. *(He makes up and down movements with his hand.)* The longer the diving board, the more it bounces throwing you higher and allowing you to make a magnificent dive.

How do your ideas come to you and how do they take shape? Do they come by chance or are they the result of long, deep reflection?

It depends on the situation. The idea may come from a thorough analysis; you see for example that you have no products in a certain price range. Then again, ideas can also come by chance, things just seen or heard. Ideas can also come from the past, from competitors or from other fields of business.

When it comes to correcting an employee, do you react in the heat of the moment or later, after cooling down?

If it is serious, I cool down first; if it is something small, I say what I have to say at the time. Generally, the more the more serious the subject, the longer I take to decide, because I have learned that the soup is not eaten at the same temperature that it is cooked at. In serious situations; taking time to think is important.

What are the keys to successful negotiation?

It is imperative to listen to the other person; a large number of negotiations fail because of a lack of receptiveness and understanding. Negotiations that succeed are a result of consensus, which is nothing more than understanding each other.

Dare to Doubt

Still on the decision-making process, what about doubt?

Doubt must always be present, even after the decision is taken. Indeed, a decision must always be questioned: nothing is ever final. We must constantly be able to adapt and doubt is an antidote to inertia. It is your best ally because it will make you question and think more deeply and thoroughly. Doubt is my friend. Those who do not doubt are dangerous.

Accept failure and learn from every mistake

For you, it is essential not to penalize failure, as without failure there is no success. In this regard you allude to major sporting champions who fail thousands of times before winning.

It is by a series of failures that children learn balance and eventually walking. We will move forward only through a succession of errors and failures. Because failure is the only way forward, we are destined to forgive. Now all our education is – alas – based on reprimand for failure. I tell my colleagues: "Make many mistakes while you are young, that way you will need to make them later" But obviously, we must never, ever, ever make the same mistake twice. In such cases I give the employee a glowing reference and send him to the competition: it is there that he will be most useful to me!

Obviously, success needs to rewarded. But should effort be rewarded, even if unsuccessful?

Of course; one can even reward failure because failure is educational. The reward must recognise the effort whether the result is failure or success. We must reward the three, effort, failure and success, but of course differently. A failure forgiven and explained is itself a reward: you learn from failure.

Each quarter I hold what I like to call the "errors meeting"! Each person has to explain one or two mistakes he has made. As spontaneously admitting mistakes is difficult at first, to "prime the pump", I give 1000 euros per mistake! There are five of us; with two errors identified each every quarter: we identify forty errors a year. Forty mistakes you do not make again! There is another point to these "errors meetings": in externalizing his or her mistakes, each person sets themselves free and everyone benefits from the missteps of others. By exchanging failures, we can improve.

Specifically, how does your idea of failure, affect the recruitment of your close associates?

For me the importance of error is such, that knowing the type of errors made is one of my recruitment criteria. I say to candidates: "Beyond all that you put forward in your resume and what you say, what mistakes have you made in the past? Small mistakes do not interest me; medium neither. Tell me your big mistakes like that, I know you do not repeat them with!me" *(Huge burst of laughter.)*

Some candidates have put their case and failed. Instead of simply eliminating them, I study their track record sympathetically. I understand difficulties, whether or not they are overcome. They deserve as much attention as the successes. Those who have had great success sometimes frighten me. Because success often breeds overconfidence. I think of the racing driver who, suddenly, because he is very busy and confident, no longer follows his checklist. Some have been so successful that they no longer doubt themselves; they can become dangerous.

You define courage as "taking the risk of being wrong" and you like to quote from Albert Einstein thoughts about error.

When asked what he wanted until the end of his life, Einstein replied: "I want to be wrong as often as possible because making mistakes is proportional to the volume of activity." But he added: "But I also hope that the consequences of each of my mistakes are infinitely small, which means that I become wise."

Undertake, discover, learn

As you know Antoine Riboud, founder of Danone, said "We must learn to understand and learn to change,". I imagine that you agree.

Of course ! Only the living dead no longer learn. Learning keeps you young. The learner cannot age. Learning typically characterizes the young. You are only old when you think you have nothing to learn.

For the Hublot Mag Bang, you put together employees from different generations: the young of course – one of whom had not even finished his studies – and retirees who brought their experience. This is a completely original policy.

I have worked with people over 70 years old, for example, a professor of metallurgy (Lucien Trueb), a production manager (René Maillefer) and a wonderful sales manager for the Middle East, my friend Jacques Tedeschi. I always made sure to work with experienced and inexperienced people. A start-up has extraordinary strength: it brings together young people who are passionate, who work round the clock, who sleep in a sleeping bag in the office, who have a crazy creativity. But these young people often have little experience. Hence the idea to add one or two pensioners who bring their forty years of experience.

At the inauguration of the LMVH Watchmaking School in 2016 in the workshops of the TAG Heuer factory in La Chaux-de-Fonds, you began by kneeling before the twelve apprentices of the first class and you said: "The is the image of the future: the old, kneeling before the generation of tomorrow!"

It's logical. These young people will take over from us. Let's help them; let's transmit our skills to them; let's put them in the saddle. This is one of our missions.

We must be constantly alert, listening. How do you apply this principle in your business day to day?

You cannot learn if you do not listen. But few people are able to listen. To listen is to show respect and humility. In a meeting, you soon tell who is listening: it takes just five minutes to see.

11

„Doing a Biver"

Mastering the art of communication

Putting the ABC of communication into practice

Gérard Lelarge: Your different passions frequently put you in the media. You are a producer of cheese, a great wine lover, a collector of watches, a defender of Swiss traditions, etc. and not just as a boss of Hublot or president of LVMH's watchmaking division. Yet brands are always mentioned. This is a particularly clever form of corporate communication, which does not cost the company a cent.

Jean-Claude Biver: During my interviews and in my lectures, I often put forward my "three commandments" (share, respect, forgive). I am often called to talk about ethical behaviour, and in this context, I obviously cites examples which refer to Hublot. Here's another example: when I speak of Swiss traditions, I mention that I produce cheese; for me the fact of making cheese is a return to the roots, since watchmaking was born on farms, where farmers became watchmakers during the winter. Over time, some of those dairy farmers who had made cheese began to just make watches. Talking about and making cheese is nothing other than a connection with the beginning of Swiss watchmaking.

By the end 2013, I had given about 60 lectures, an average of slightly more than one per week; particularly to students, because I need and want to pass on my life-lessons and my experiences. I sometimes had three conferences in one day. Most are in English or

German. I gave numerous lectures at the IMD in Lausanne, Tsinghua University in Beijing, the London Business School, INSEAD in Paris, or in Boston at Harvard Business School. Fortunately, I do not need to prepare; I know how to speak without notes!

Communicate authentically and pragmatically

During your lectures, you tell stories, you laugh, you charm. To use your words, you "do a Biver." Given the success of your lectures, you are often called a rock star. You evince your "contagious enthusiasm". What are the ingredients of your success, when faced with very different audiences?

Simplicity and authenticity: people understand what I say! I give clear messages without PowerPoint. It is livelier, more spontaneous.

Man communicates not only by what he says but also by physical and facial expressions and by what others notice about him. Being authentic is more convincing. This is what people are looking for today: someone to tell the truth from the heart. Few speakers have understood this: most speak ex cathedra, with charts, graphs; they want to show their status and intelligence. I want to show my humanity and my simplicity. I'm not an intellectual; I am pragmatic and therefore I speak in a simple and concrete way.

You have said: "I tell the truth with a little painting." What do you mean?

We must distinguish the truth of photography from truth of painting. In a painting of, say, the coves of the coast at Cassis, you will find much more emotion, more depth, more colour than in a photo, even if the painting does not accurately represent reality. The painting conveys emotions. Personally, I often put paint in my words. Purists may say that's not exactly like that. Indeed, it is not exactly like that, but that's how I tell it to you.

In front of an audience who have come to listen to you talk about watches, sometimes you say nothing on the subject, but talk about cheese and taste it too. It is a method of communication that is at the very least original and daring. And it works well. How do you explain this paradox?

There is nothing worse than listening to someone trying to sell you something systematically. When a speaker mentions the name of his company ten times, you no longer want to listen. I always do the opposite and say nothing about the watch brands I oversee, or talk about it for only thirty seconds.

In 2006, you created Hublot TV, the first Internet TV channel created by a luxury brand.

Once again, the goal was to be the first, different and unique. We understood very quickly that to be visited, the website must evolve every day. The goal is to try to show something new every day, whatever it is, and sometimes it may not be directly related to us: an exhibition in Bern, a festival in Geneva, etc.

Each year we have 8 million unique visitors each spending on average five minutes: that's nearly 400 000 hours per year. Beyond that, we made sure to use the fastest and the best social networks, as we immediately grasped their importance.

Personalized partnerships

Successful partnerships implemented at Omega and Hublot are based largely on personal relationships that you forged with celebrities. With what alchemy enables you to connect to continue that closeness with people as different as Cindy Crawford or Diego Maradona?

We were pioneers in this field. The idea is not just to be content with using the picture of our "ambassadors" alongside our watches, but to share with them. We ask them to come to our exhibitions, our press conferences, and events that we organize.

For an ambassador to come with me to China, he or she must want to come, and he or she will want to come if he understands what we do, provided the brand and the watch create emotion. It is this specific relationship that allows us to have much impact and to work in depth with our ambassadors. You can imagine that in China a press conference with Cindy Crawford has more impact than a press conference with Biver! Working with an ambassador is not just about buying the rights to a photo, but to create an advocate for the brand. This is what we did with Hublot ambassador Bar Rafaeli, particularly in the context of the women's Big Bang Broderie collection a watch born from the fusion of the Swiss tradition of embroidery (from embroidery factory Bischoff) and the high technology that allowed Hublot to claim a world first and make a case, dial and bracelet that was entirely embroidered!

TAG Heuer, was associated in particular with Steve McQueen, and has had partnerships with many celebrities Leonardo DiCaprio, Brad Pitt, Cameron Diaz, Tiger Woods, Ronaldo, Maria Sharapova, Tom Brady, Kei Nishikori. Early in 2015 the brand announced a new ambassador: the young British supermodel Cara Delevingne who has appeared in shows for many top designers. Why this association?

Simply because there is consistency between the image of TAG Heuer, a disruptor brand of today aimed a young, connected crowd; and the image of Cara, sassy, bold, brazen. A total *It Girl!*

While the business world is in part rational, logical, cold, and impersonal, lot of business is done through the friendship and closeness you have with your contacts. Not everyone is able to establish personal relationships with ambassadors.

Exactly. We must be able to fit into the lifestyle of our ambassador. I played golf with George Clooney in Cannes-Mandelieu;

you have to know how to talk to him. I personally have the ability to adapt to different environments, without anxiety and embarrassment even though I do not live the same lifestyle. But the fact that I am authentic and natural really makes me different from my competitors; that's why it works.

The exclusive partnerships formed in 2014 included one between Hublot and the American football team the Dallas Cowboys, and another between Zenith and the Rolling Stones, about which there was much press … with pictures not only of yourself but of course also your young son with rock stars!

This partnership was finalised during the launch of the Zenith El Primero Chronomaster 1969, of which we made 250 examples with a dial featuring the group's logo: the famous tongue with red lips. Beyond the worldwide fame of our ambassadors, it is worth remembering that from a technical point of view we created for a movement for this watch, that measures tenths of a second!

12

"1 + 1 = 3"

Synergies unleashed

Developing the desirability of the brand

Gérard Lelarge: Establishing partnerships with the beautiful people accelerates the desirability of the brand and provides years of visibility. Let's take the example of the "My choice" campaign with Cindy Crawford. How did this campaign for Omega come about?

Jean-Claude Biver: Omega launched this campaign for the Constellation model. At one point in the design process, Cindy gave her opinion on the various projects; therefore, the watch was indeed "her choice". Today, if you say "My choice" in China, the Chinese see a watch. This campaign was so strong and credible because it was authentic.

How did the partnership with Omega and James Bond come about and what was your strategy?

For the film GoldenEye, released in 1995 with Pierce Brosnan, it was proposed that we pay a few thousand dollars for James Bond to wear Omega. As I was convinced of the need to establish a relationship that maximised the synergies, that is to say to make 1 + 1 = 3, we offered the amount we were originally asked for, plus a few hundred thousand dollars more. In return we received a significant number of additional rights, such as making films of 15, 30 and 45 seconds, and photos taken on set during filming.

We also had the right to advertise with the actor wearing an Omega six months before the film was released and six months after it had left the market; in other words a relatively long period. We were also with the actors on the film launch tour and could participate in all events organized around the film. With all these activities, we succeeded in making the public aware was James Bond was wearing the Omega Seamaster 007. Before they had even gone to see the film.

You also managed to revive the so-called "moonwatch", the Omega Speedmaster, originally designed for motor racing.

Indeed. Omega was not chosen by chance by NASA in 1965: NASA had purchased a large number of Swiss watches, the Speedmaster was tested and was found to be the best. In Neil Armstrong we had the best ambassador in the world. He also was a free ambassador since the Americans had bought the watches that they then loaned to astronauts during their missions! In the early 1990s, we revived the space adventure in which Omega was a key player, especially with the Journey of Apollo 13 in 1970. The computer system crashed, Houston had to manually start retro rockets and run them for 12 seconds exactly. The astronaut had to start his chronograph and stop after 12 seconds. The watch played a crucial role in this adventure; which could have ended tragically. This has been boon for Omega's history. As well as Apollo the Speedmaster was also on board Gemini, and Skylab.

Is it true that Neil Armstrong left his watch inside the spacecraft?

It is true that the first moonwalk on that famous July 21, 1969, Neil Armstrong was not wearing the watch and Buzz Aldrin put it on for the second moonwalk. I asked Neil Armstrong how it felt to wear a watch on the moon. He said that this was part of the procedure: the watch, secured with Velcro, was part of the official clothing; and if something went wrong it could be used to overcome a technical failure as it did with Apollo 13. Armstrong also told me that having a watch on the wrist in space and then on the Moon was the only thing that linked him to the Earth. Nothing reminded him of planet Earth, except the watch.

For your advertising campaigns, you used the moon buggy on the streets of New York, Tokyo, Shanghai…, again demonstrating your ability to astonish in order to better communicate.

This vehicle now seems completely obsolete. One wonders how they did it: no one would cross a field in such a thing, let alone the surface of the moon! Of course our drives in the street were events that generated a lot of curiosity.

Minimizing risk…

Hublot developed a programme of sports sponsorship. This is doubly logical. First because it concerns the timing and time measurement, but also because there are similarities between luxury watches and sports. For example the ever-present concern about performance and being overtaken as well as the aesthetic dimension in reference to the beauty of the movement of a champion. My question is this: are these the similarities that have led you to participate in various sports events? Could you imagine an association with cultural events like opera or classical concerts?

Sport is a universal language. It is therefore an essential driver of awareness. Each year Hublot spends about 8 to 10 % of its turnover in sports sponsorship. If no luxury brand was associated with the cultural world, it is very likely that we would have done. We did not go there because the field was already crowded, as is the case for golf competitions, horse riding and tennis. So we deliberately chose areas where we could say again: 'we will be first, different and unique' – provided there is consistency between the events we sponsor and what we are. To be first, different and unique is idiotic if there is no consistency with your DNA.

In terms of sports sponsorship, your policy is to partner with sports events that cannot lose. As you write so amusingly, sponsoring an event, you are "certain to reach the final" and "never be associated with defeat."

That's right. For example, we rarely associate with footballers who are still playing, but with those who no longer play, that is to say legends like the king, Pele. Hublot was involved with two soccer World Cups (2010 in South Africa and 2014 in Brazil), Euro 2008 and Euro 2016. The brand is also the official timekeeper of Chelsea and PSG. We are also associated with teams like Bayern Munich. These teams have become brands and legends; like Ferrari for example; regardless of the result. The audience attracted to big football matches is enormous: about 900 million households in 190 countries watch the most important ones.

"Hublot loves football" is one of your messages on sponsorship. What was your strategy during the World Cup in Brazil in 2014, event at which you have hosted more than 1200 guests?

First, on 12 June 2013, Hublot unveiled a countdown clock on Copacabana Beach, 365 days before the start of the Cup. Hublot was the official timekeeper throughout and received exceptional media exposure. The Brazil "Mundial" 1 was viewed 40 billion times. We sponsored the referees' board and designed it as a watch ... but with a third cut out so for visibility! This appeared on average 12 to 15 seconds per game, totalling 22 minutes of visibility worldwide. During the 2014 Cup, we had nearly 3 million visitors to our site, against about 300 000 each month. Finally, so that our guests had an unforgettable memory of this event we took over a 100-room hotel in Copacabana.

Hublot was also the official watch of the Euro 2016.

Produced in an edition of only a hundred, the Big Bang Euro 2016 was designed to time the game to the minute. It measures the length of a match (twice 45 minutes) and the additional time and the centre of the window shows the period of the current match. As for the World Cup in 2014 or the UEFA Champions League, Hublot designed the board of the 4th special referee for Euro 2016.

Your strategy includes being highly selective in signing particularly high performance athletes. I refer of course to Usain Bolt.

Since 2007, Hublot's ambassador has indeed been the fastest man in the world! We created the King Power Usain Bolt and produced a series of 250 watches. The strap of the watch is the same colour as his shoes. Usain suggested that to us; he said, "I have a colour that Puma has developed for me: a slightly metallic gold, perhaps you could use it for the strap." Which is what we have done.

Always exploring new paths

Hublot has developed sponsorship activities in sailing, F1, polo, golf, skiing… sports whose image corresponds well enough to that of a luxury company. But since 2008, Hublot has also sponsored football; this could seem surprising. Is a luxury brand – offering products not accessible to the "common man" – not at risk of confusing its image by associating with a popular sport?

Originally, you did not see any luxury bands in football any luxury brand. This sport is the prerogative of mass sponsors or companies that sell consumer goods at very affordable prices.

We entered football for three reasons. First: football is a popular sport, which interests many people: men and women, young and old, rich and poor. This is what I call the "verticality" of football. Second: Who are the owners of football clubs? Billionaires: think of Agnelli and Juventus, Berlusconi and AC Milan, and Qatar and PSG. More than that players, coaches, and staff are all potential Hublot customers. Third: the influence of footballers on young people is enormous; they are celebrities, heroes, just like movie stars; they are excellent influencers. Therefore, you can see a very high degree of consistency between Hublot and the world of football. Be first, different and unique, in this case being the first luxury watchmaker to invest in this sport is conceivable only if it is compatible with our DNA. And this is even more the case with Hublot which mainly manufactures sports and lifestyle watches.

Betting on the customer of tomorrow

In addition, in sponsoring football, you bet on the future, via a public of young people who might be future customers.

Indeed, football allows us to work on the customers of tomorrow. Hublot is already in the memories of these young people as a kind of icon. Football speaks to those who can buy now, to those who can buy tomorrow and also to those who will never buy; but not in an irritating way. In the *favelas* of Brazil, all the kids know Ferrari and wear Ferrari caps. The fact that the vast majority of people will never buy a Ferrari does not diminish the prestige of the brand.

This partnership with football illustrates the originality and boldness of your approach. Engaging in football reflects your ability to grasp new opportunities before everyone else. Sponsorship of football is a win-win partnership: Hublot opens a window to on the world of luxury for football; and in return you receive support for certain markets. This is for instance the case of Manchester United vis-à-vis China.

Manchester United is a club that is revered in Asia. It is not just a football team, it is a myth, as is FC Bayern, Juventus or PSG. So, the impact of all activities with these clubs is enormous. Once again, we were innovative because few people understood why we partner with the team of an industrial city particularly affected by the crisis.

Your success vis-à-vis football gives ideas to competitors. How do you react to this?

We are happy when we see competitors following suit! This allows us to assert ourselves as a leader. A leader without a follower is not a leader.

Betting on both Maradona and Ferrari

Beyond the originality of your approach to partnership with the football world, it was also pretty daring to bet on Maradona at a time when his image was tarnished as a controversial figure.

Our approach may seem bold seen in Europe where Maradona had a dubious reputation. But we did not sign him to sell watches in France and Germany! We took Maradona to South America, Asia and the Middle East. In Asia, he is a SUPERSTAR and his reputation is intact.

The partnership with Maradona led to two watches: the Big Bang Maradona in 2010 and the King Power in 2012, both sold in limited edition.

Maradona has such personality that the limited editions we have made with him enjoyed huge success. For example, for the first limited series of 250 watches, we had nearly 2000 applications (of course we only made 250). It was one of the most requested watches in our history. Each came with the No 10 (his number) shirt of the Argentine squad. He signed 250 shirts; it took him four hours. We then made a second series, at his suggestion, with his signature and the number 10 engraved on the watch.

During Euro 2016 Maradona and Pele participated symbolically in an opening match but the most important moment of the year was the meeting of Maradona with Pope Francis.

Diego Maradona participated in a charity match the at the Vatican organized at the pontiff's initiative for peace in the world. For this occasion, Hublot created a dedicated model – the Big Bang Unico United for Peace – a unique piece that Maradona has personally presented to Pope Francis. This watch was later auctioned to help the victims of earthquakes in Italy.

In the area of sailing, as in other types of sponsorship, you create a real partnership. With Alinghi you explained that you were not "on the boat" but "with the boat": defending the values of Switzerland and showing your sense of solidarity at a time when other sponsors – including Audemars Piguet – withdrew.

The rules of the "America's Cup" are strict: all the components of a Swiss boat must be manufactured in Switzerland. The project aimed to show all the technological skills of the country, Hublot needed to be part of this, as an actor anxious to defend *"Swiss made"*. It is also worth remembering that Hublot was the official timekeeper of the 2013 Bol d'Or, the most important regatta in Switzerland and most prestigious in an enclosed body of water anywhere in the world. Once again you see the idea of sponsoring an event, rather than a team that could be associated with a defeat.

In Formula 1, Hublot is working alongside the Ayrton Senna Foundation in Brazil.

It's a great story. In 2006, I met Viviane Senna, Ayrton's sister, to ask permission to use her brother's image. She replied that this image belongs to the Ayrton Senna Institute, a foundation to get children out of slums and poverty. To snatch them from the world of crime and drugs, there is only one solution: education. I found this a great idea: when you give money to underprivileged children, they spend it; when you give them education, you pull them out of the world of crime and poverty. Since its inception, the foundation has funded years of schooling for millions of children. In return for its financial support, Hublot can use the signature and photo of Ayrton Senna. With each special series – there have been four since 2006 – a significant amount goes directly to the foundation. Finally, in 2013, Hublot created a watch stamped Ayrton Senna, made in a limited series of 41 in just three materials, referencing Brazilian champion's three titles and 41 wins.

Omega first involvement in F1 dates back to 1996 with Michael Schumacher, at a time when he was not yet world champion … which reveals a certain flair!

More precisely a certain capacity for anticipation, is indispensable to the manager. he must constantly anticipate and he does with his experience and his instincts. We should always try to have an edge. That's what we did with Michael Schumacher, we signed a partnership when he drove for Benetton, speculating that he would one day drive for Ferrari.

One of the peculiarities of Hublot is taking a brand as an ambassador. How did the partnership with Ferrari come about?

When the Big Bang was created in 2005, I immediately thought of Ferrari. I showed it to Jean Todt who found it sensational. But at the time Hublot was hardly known and the board of Ferrari declined our offer. In 2011, I was in St. Tropez, where I met Lapo Elkann, heir of Fiat and grandson of Giovanni Agnelli. Lapo said, "Listen, Hublot and Ferrari should do something together." He organized a lunch in Maranello, hometown of Ferrari, with the directors. Over lunch, we offered a "360 degree" partnership agreement, and not just the creation of a Hublot watch with Ferrari's logo on it.

Your goal is, to use your expression, "to enter the world Ferrari."

We actually partner classic cars and sports cars (Scuderia). And Hublot showcases are at all exhibitions and in all the showrooms of the dealer network as well as being present at Ferrari clubs and at every new car launch.

In 2011 you signed a five-year contract with Ferrari, which is a long time.

Our aim is to initiate long term strategies over many years and not to work in a hurry, which would be the case when you know that a contract expires in eighteen months. Another example of our 'long contract' policy is our arrangement with the World Cup: Hublot is a partner until 2022.

In 2012, a Hublot manufactured a watch to celebrate the 50th anniversary of the Ferrari 250 GTO.

The GTO is a legendary car, only 36 were built during the early 1960s, and it is the billionaires' favourite car; I recently heard of one for sale for more than $ 55 000 000 For each owner, we manufactured a watch with the chassis number engraved on the movement. We did the same for the new Ferrari Enzo.

The MP-05 LaFerrari of 2013 was described by the press as "strange UFO watchmaking."

This watch, the first fully conceived, designed and developed by Hublot's engineers and watchmakers working with the Ferrari team, obviously pays tribute to the Italian manufacturer's most recent racing car of the Italian manufacturer. The movement is built along the lines of the architecture of the famous V12 Ferrari. It is hand-wound and it has a power reserve of fifty days; in other words it does not need to be wound for 1200 hours, which is an historic world record and makes it the watch with longest power reserve. The previous record stood at forty days.

Betting on basketball and boxing

Hublot has a partnership with basketball through Dwyane Wade who in 2012 became NBA champion. It is also the official timekeeper of the American Airlines Arena, and the partner of Miami Heat.

Basketball is to the US that soccer is in Europe. One day we saw Dwayne Wade with a Hublot on the wrist; this gave us the idea to contact him! As we did for Diego Maradona and Usain Bolt.

On the subject of boxing, there was an exceptional evening in September 2012 with the World Boxing Council, in Las Vegas, during which twelve watches were auctioned to benefit a relief fund for boxers who have retired from the ring. Can you say a few words about this sponsorship?

The billionaire Carlos Slim created a foundation to help former boxers, some of whom experience hard times after their careers in the ring have ended. The idea of helping appealed us. We proposed to Jose Sulaiman, head of the WBC, that we manufacture twelve unique watches honouring twelve legendary boxers. And the twelve watches were auctioned, during a party at which buyers and boxers sat together at the same tables.

At the opening of the 50th congress of the WBC in December 2012, you received the title of "Man of the Year" for your humanitarian commitment to boxing – a particularly important honour.

I considered it a great honour; the more so because in the past the distinction of "Man of the Year" was awarded to Nelson Mandela and to Carlos Slim. Another source of satisfaction – one more important than my personal pride – was the fact that the sale of twelve Hublot watches that we offer raised over a million dollars; paid in full to the WBC.

Remaining on the subject of boxing, in 2016 TAG Heuer started a five-year partnership honouring Muhammad Ali. After his death in June 2016 we launched a special series of watches ("Tribute to Muhammad Ali") and organized an evening party as a tribute to the champion with a charity auction which raised $ 100 000 for the Muhammad Ali Center.

At the beginning of 2015 the young pianist Lang Lang become a Hublot "ambassador". Why?

We partnered with someone who is considered a demigod in China and who is famous beyond his international reputation as a virtuoso pianist, he played during the opening ceremony of the FIFA World Cup 2006 in Munich, then in 2014 in Rio, at the 2008 Olympic games in Beijing and at the World Expo in Shanghai in 2010. He has collaborated with UNICEF and was named "messenger of peace" by the UN in 2013. Lang Lang fits perfectly with the philosophy of Hublot; combining tradition and the future.

What other partnerships were recently initiated by the watchmaking division of LVMH, which you now lead?

TAG Heuer, which is already associated with Formula 1, golf, tennis, sailing, football, is now moving towards cycling, music and lifestyle. For its part, Zenith became official timekeeper and partner of the Tour Auto, and classic car and motorcycle rallies and races.. At the beginning of 2015 Hublot partnered with Justin Rose, winner of 17 world titles, including the US Open Golf Championship in 2013. We also entered the poker world as the official timekeeper of the World Poker Tour in Las Vegas. Again we were first, different and unique! We also associate with cricket competitions, a very popular sport in India, Australia, the Middle East and all countries of the Commonwealth; which gives us coverage across four continents. Finally Hublot is the official partner of the Grande Odyssée Savoie Mont Blanc 2015, which is an international dogsled race across the most uneven territory in the world (over a course of hundreds of kilometres with a total change in altitude of 20 000 cumulative meters. As you see, our areas of operation are varied because above all we want to follow our client; to be present wherever he finds himself and be part of his world and his lifestyle.

13

"TAG is cool. Hublot and Zenith too."

Renewal through preservation of DNA

Daring to launch a connected watch

Gérard Lelarge: In November 2015 TAG Heuer launched its first connected watch, in partnership with Intel and Google. The launch took place in New York in the presence of: Bernard Arnault, LVMH CEO; Brian Krzanich, president of Intel; David Singleton, vice president of Google and of course yourself, the originator of this project. Why does a luxury watch brand as, let's say, "traditional" as Tag Heuer, choose to associate itself with companies so symbols of new technology companies?

Jean-Claude Biver: The partnership with Intel and Google became necessary for us, as a watchmaker, to have access to all the technology (hardware and software) necessary for making a connected watch ourselves.

Beyond this technical issue, by proposing a TAG Heuer at 1500 dollars, we aim to protect our entry price against competition from other connected watches. It also allows us to attract new buyers who, without this connected watch, would never have been customers; and the connected watch may well be a springboard to the future acquisition of a mechanical watc. So for luxury watch brands both types of watches, mechanical and connected, are more complementary than competitive.

What are the features of this connected watch?

First, it looks nothing like the Apple Watch as we have not sought to copy it, our goal, again, is to be first, different and unique. The model on which we based the TAG Heuer Connected is the Carrera, a great classic of our brand. Its case, made of titanium, is almost identical to that of the watch created in 1963. When I wear it no one notices that the watch on my wrist is a connected watch. A TAG Heuer should look like a TAG Heuer; and not a computer. We renew ourselves by protecting our DNA.

To return to the features of this watch, it can display messages, sports results, the distance travelled by its owner, the rhythm of his heartbeat, an itinerary, etc., etc. Thousands of applications can be downloaded using Android Wear, the Google operating system.

Finally, and highly originally, we found a way to make this connected watch "eternal"! After two years, the owner can bring it back to the shop and, paying difference of the original price, leave with a mechanical Carrera. In other words, you can buy a luxury watch for only 2700 euros.

You mean that this watch will never be obsolete.

Indeed. As already noted, a mechanical watch is by nature eternal. In a thousand years, it will still work. Watchmaking is synonymous with art and eternity. On the contrary a connected watch becomes obsolete after four or five years; except our TAG Heuer Connected, since we can always exchange it against a mechanical watch; an advantage that only a watchmaker can offer. After all, we are watchmakers and not computer manufacturers!

The TAG Heuer Connected launched at the end of 2015 did not have the "Swiss made" label. Why, in your eyes, is this a disadvantage?

To obtain the famous magic words "Swiss made" watch components must be manufactured and assembled in Switzerland. That said, for connected watches, the "Swiss made" is much less important than people say; clients do not care whether these two words appear on the face of their watch or not. Nevertheless, our TAG Heuer Connected is both "Swiss engineered" (first asset) and has "Intel inside" – the microprocessor is Intel – (second asset).

Since 1st January 2017 the rules of the "Swiss made" have been strengthened. What about this reform?

Today 60 % of the value in terms of product and technical development of the watch and the movement must be carried out in Switzerland to earn the epithet Swiss Made.

We want to see the integrated manufacture of our connected watch in this country.. So with Intel we are going to set up a production unit in La Chaux-de-Fonds, traditional stronghold of watchmaking, to assemble microprocessors at TAG Heuer. This will be a real transfer of technology.

Since its launch the TAG Heuer connected watch has enjoyed great success, including among a rather traditional clientele attached to the mechanical watch.

Indeed. We planned to sell 20 000 watches per year; we exceeded 50 000. Online sales of the watch were suspended for a while and the production rate was increased to meet demand. The brand, which outperforms the industry average, quickly smashed all projections. We expect to sell 150 000 connected watches in 2017. This success gives new impetus, and a new image to Tag Heuer. The brand, which aims at younger customers than in the past (the partnership with Cristiano Ronaldo as brand ambassador is significant in this respect) is now seen as cool.

Because we only started there in 2011 we have a lot of ground to catch up, we actually opened sixty points of sale in China in 2016 and will open as many in 2017. Moreover, TAG Heuer has become a partner of the China National Space Administration, CNSA, which is planning to send a robot mission to Mars in 2020. We also became the sponsor of Chinese Football league.

Do you think that the Swiss watch industry in particular, which has seen its *exports fall,* and whose successes are made only at the expense of the market shares of competitors, should bet on new connected watches.

It is imperative to bet on this new technology. Soon it will be everywhere. We will be increasingly surrounded by items of information technology that communicate among themselves. The smartphone will become obsolete very rapidly. This is one reason why companies like Apple are also active on the connected watch market.

The Swiss watch industry should not underestimate the impact of this type of watch and therefore miss a market that is beginning to develop. To say that the Apple Watch is not a watch is a mistake: we must take the Apple brand seriously. More than twelve million connected watches will be sold each year and Swiss watchmakers are obviously threatened by competitors in the price segment up to about 1500 euros. Hence the importance and the urgency of responding to this new challenge. Otherwise the Swiss watch industry will continue to lose market share.

It is imperative to build on the success of connected watches; consumers seek high-end versions of new technology. A luxury market is created the moment customers want to differentiate themselves from the majority. Swiss prestige, know-how, and quality undoubtedly allow us to master this segment.

In your opinion do connected watches coming out of Switzerland rival those by Apple and Samsung ?

This is essential. We will also open an office in Silicon Valley. Producing a connected watch without a presence in this mythical location would be as absurd as couturier working the fashion business without being present in Paris or Milan.

At the Swiss watch fair Baselworld 2016, you launched a new model: the Carrera TAG Heuer CH02T with a tourbillon.

Evidently this is a tehnical gem at an unbeatable price. A skeleton tourbillon watch is usually between 60 000 and 80 000 euros. Ours is sold for less than 15 000 euros. The reason is simple: our watch is made using 21st century technology. Once again, we see the importance of research and innovation.

In March 2017, you launched a new Carrera Connected! What are the features of this watch?

It includes a GPS chip, a more powerful battery, a faster chip, better reception and improved screen. It will be available in several sizes, including a small one aimed at women. Important assets for capturing an even larger number of customers!! *(Great laughter).*

Will Hublot also launch a connected watch?

Yes, in 2018 or 2019, but with a difference: in order not to lose their soul as luxury mechanical watches, the technology will not be integrated inside the case but on the wristband or in an additional case.

Innovating again and again

Tag Heuer continues its policy of innovation policy to promote Carrera Connected for instance presenting very original dials.

Innovation is actually part of the DNA of TAG Heuer. I keep it in mind that TAG means Techniques d'Avant Garde Beyond technology, we innovate in the field of design. For instance ten new dials were designed by several brand ambassadors; among them Cristiano Ronaldo, Tom Brady, David Guetta, Jessica Korda and The Nervo Sisters.

And an eleventh dial that you yourself have done, with the word LOVE.

Yes. A word that is dear to me. All these dials are available for owners of a Carrera Connected and can be downloaded. We should soon be seeing new versions of the watch including one in gold version and a diamond-set version in 2017.

Still on the subject of innovation will Tag Heuer intensify online sales of watches?

Consumer habits are changing and we have to go where the consumer goes. That way we can attract the next generation of buyers. Young people who are now between 15 and 20 buy books and clothes online. Tomorrow, when they are between 25 and 30, they will find it completely normal to buy a luxury watch online.

In the United States Tag Heuer has already made a start by distributing its new watch on the Internet. The connected watch is ideal product to sell online.

In 2015 Zenith began online sales too, becoming the first high end Swiss watch company to offer its products through a solely online dealer.

In terms of sports sponsorship TAG Heuer, like Hublot, is developing its activities in the world of football.

We are the official timekeeper for German, Spanish and English football championships. We signed a partnership with Manchester United, as you know, one of the best soccer teams in the world. In 2016 the *Premier League,* the English Football Championship, chose TAG Heuer as the official timekeeper. Thus, the brand logo, visible on the referee's board, appeared in all TV broadcasts.

Tag Heuer is also present in the world of motor racing.

In this way we were able to revive our famous slogan of the 90s: *"Don't crack under pressure."* We support the Formula 1 team Red Bull Racing, which has been renamed "Red Bull Racing RB12 TAG Heuer." We are thus Official Timekeeper and Official Watch of the team.

With Hublot you were an early-adopter of football. You are now in cycling with TAG Heuer.

That's correct. Cycling is now the new favourite sport of top managers. Hublot was copied when it became involved with football, TAG Heuer is now pioneering cycling. Today people are surprised. Tomorrow we will be copied! *(Big laugh).* Once again we lead the way. TAG Heuer is now associated with the BMC Racing team. This is overseen by my brother Marc, who was boss of the Tour de Suisse and the Tour de Romandie. This is the second time a luxury watchmaker has been involved in cycling … I understand that as early as 80s and 90s TAG Heuer was a sponsor of Team 7-Eleven. Synergies are possible between BMC and TAG Heuer: BMC offers high quality avant-garde products; plus we share the same values and have the same types of customers.

Transmitting to new generations

In 2016, in partnership with the Institute of Craft Excellence (l'Institut des Métiers de l'Excellence or IME) created in 2014 by LVMH, TAG Heuer and Zenith founded the School of Horology in the TAG Heuer factory in La Chaux-de -Funds. Can you tell us the aims and the originality of this approach?

To be clear, the aim of the IME is to perpetuate artisanal crafts through apprenticeship training programs run by different companies within the LMVH group. It is of course a policy that enables transmission of expertise, but also it promotes equality of opportunity. The originality of our common training program at TAG Heuer and Zenith (created with Chantal Gaemperle, HR and Executive Committee member of the group) is to provide entry to the fields of artisanal crafts, design and sales. The idea is no longer to be an apprentice with TAG Heuer in La Chaux-de-Fonds, but to be an apprentice with LVMH across the world. These young people can change the country, jobs, and brands throughout their careers. Training qualifications are available to them, in 16 skills areas ranging from watches to leather goods or wine, through marketing.

14

"One day I told my wife I wanted to make cheese."

Back to basics: cultivating authenticity

Gérard Lelarge: Let us now turn to a passion that seems very original: making cheese! Nonetheless, cheese and watches are intimately linked since luxury watchmaking in Switzerland began on farms.

Jean-Claude Biver: It is part of our rural heritage: French Protestants, the Huguenots, fleeing persecution by Catholics took refuge in Switzerland and they found skills important for watchmaking among the farmers of the Jura. During the winter they entrusted the delicate tasks of cutting or polishing these to these meticulous, extremely patient peasants. Some farmers wanted to continue during the summer and they became "farmer watchmakers". Then one day they left their farms to become full time watchmakers. Of course, I do not make my cheese personally and nor do I herd my cows … any more than I myself manufacture watches! But my activity in the field of cheese allows me to connect with the source of my work. Symbolically, for the opening of the Hublot Vendôme store in Paris in 2011, which was attended by Alain Delon, we brought cows and a party was held with cheese fondue, Swiss wines.

A cheese that tastes of flowers …

What are the characteristics of your cheese? You often explain that your milk has a particular taste thanks to the fact that in the pastures cows eat flowers.

I wanted my cheese to be of exceptional quality, the high price is irrelevant because I do not sell it. It is cooked over a wood fire using milk from cows that graze when flowers bloom in the meadows, giving it that special taste. Flowering begins in the plains; from mid-May we bring the cows to pastures at 1000 meters altitude, where the first flowers appear. Then we take them up to 1400 meters and, on about September 20 when flowering finishes, we go back down the plain. We make our cheese during these four months, from mid-May to mid-September. In the pasture of the Neuvaz, at 1300 meters above sea level, we have a large 800 litre copper pot and every day we produce on average 1000 litres of milk from which we produce about 90 kilograms of cheese. It is then brought down to the plains and matures in cellars where it is rubbed daily with a damp cloth and a little salt. The first cheese can be eaten from mid-December. Our herd allows us to produce about 4500 kilos of cheese a year.

You serve your cheese in a variety of situations. You auction it for the benefit of associations, such as the Foundation of the Grand Duke and the Grand Duchess of Luxembourg who fight against all forms of exclusion and work for the integration of marginalized people. Your cheese is also a public relations tool. They say you always travel with it. What is it really about?

I give my clients cheese. It is Hublot's Christmas gift, a welcome gift since it comes from the heart. Giving this cheese says more than the gift of a beautiful silver pen or a nice tie. My cheese has gradually built an incredible reputation; and to carve out a reputation, there is nothing better than to say it is not for sale. If you want to sell something, always say it's not for sale! *(Burst of Laughter.)*

At 20, you manufactured honey; you dreamt of nature; you wanted to live on a farm. This dream has been partly fulfilled and cheese reconnects you with the Joux Valley, to which you are particularly attached.

This is one of the dreams that I have made a reality. I always dreamed of being close to nature, to have cows, make cheese, to have a farmyard.

The September 'désalpe'

Every September the désalpe, (the descent of the herd from its mountain pastures) is an essential element of the return to school. Tell me about the fun you have organizing this event, which brings together a very numerous and disparate crowd.

We bring down the cows from our pasture which is located 17 kilometres from my farm. This descent is traditionally called the désalpe. The cheesemakers, in other words the herdsmen, are pleased to return to the plains with their families as they have lived four months only in small chalets in the mountains. This descent is an opportunity for a big party. The desalpe celebrates both the return of the men, the herd and the cheese. And you could say that my farm is one of the few "city farms", since I live on the edge of town and I organize the only désalpe happens at the lakeside.

There are two important details to underline: we see no Hublot signs at the désalpe and it is the only day when you do not wear a watch.

That's right; for one simple reason: you must never use this type of tradition and culture for commercial purposes. If people make an association with Hublot, fine, but there was never a hint of Hublot branding. And when I lead the herd, I do not wear a watch, I'm dressed according to tradition; and traditionally cowherds never wore a watch on the wrist, but had pocket watches.

15

"Wine is sacred. It is the fusion between God and man."

Respect and venerate

Discovering wine

Gérard Lelarge: Your grandfather Marcel Zeien, who had a great influence in your life, introducing you to wine in Beaujolais, when you were 6 years old. He taught you to discover it, to respect it.

Jean-Claude Biver: Part of my grandmother's family were winemakers and my grandmother came from Beaujolais. My grandfather taught us, my brother Marc and me, not to "drink" wine but always to taste, to discover and try to memorize it. He especially taught us to respect it. Wine is the drink that brings people together, it is the drink of emotion, and friendship. It is the fruit of God who gives us the climate and the earth, and men who give their work. My grandfather first made us taste a drop of wine and, as and as we grew up a little more, until we had half a glass. He used to ask us, "What are we drinking?" As there was no label on the bottle, my grandmother somtimes whispered to us, telling us if it was a Brouilly, a Villages or a Moulin-à-Vent. Later, I also came to know and appreciate wine with my father and my mother; who are both great wine lovers with great palates, then I in my turn started to initiate my children in the discovery of wine.

Château d'Yquem 1811!

You started very young and your wine collection, is particularly prestigious. You have all vintages of Château d'Yquem since 1811. Can you tell us about this wine?

I bought Yquem for the first time in Codec Rousses! The store manager, Mr. Gauthier, explained that this is the greatest wine in the world and the only one you can drink after a century… while no big red Bordeaux – excluding exceptions such as Cheval Blanc 1947 – can keep more than sixty years. When I learned that a vine yielded only 10 cl of wine, and that the grapes were harvested one by one, I fell in love with this wine. As I wanted to have the vintages of my children's and my wife's birthdays, I decided to begin buying Yquem in 1967.

Beyond Yquem, what does your wine collection comprise?

Besides Cheval Blanc, which is one of the best wines in the world, I like Haut-Brion. I also like the wine of our region, the Lavaux, which is a UNESCO World Heritage site. It was the Romans who planted vines and there are several little known grape varieties that are extraordinary. In Lavaux, we use mostly Chasselas. The French eat it as a table grape but the Swiss make an exceptional wine with it. I am also the ambassador of the wines of this region and I often serve them at Hublot events

In 2014, Hublot has signed a three-year partnership with the Office of Vaud wines. What form does this partnership take?

The Office is chaired by Pierre Keller, a friend of thirty years; and the wines are the official wines of Hublot events worldwide; for instance they were served during the World Cup in Brazil.

Would you like to buy a vineyard?

I like the idea, but I have not done so at the moment, because I did not find a vineyard. There are some vineyards where I live but these are not domaines. If one day I the opportunity to purchase a domaine here comes along, I will; however, I am not interested in buying a wine producing estate abroad.

What similarities are there between a great wine and a luxury watch?

Both are timepieces and instruments of memory. Just as with luxury watches, wine requires very meticulous care. Among the points that wine and watches have in common are tradition, history, the quality of the raw material, a desire excellence, and rarity.

For you, wine can be only be enjoyed when shared.

I see wine as a product that brings people together. It cannot be drunk alone. Only alcoholics drink alone.

16

"I collect the watches with my heart."

Share and transmit

Buy with passion

Gérard Lelarge: Cheese, wine, watches. I think your collection includes a large number of Patek Philippe watches, a maker that inspires you with great respect, both for the brand and the people behind it.

Jean-Claude Biver: In my opinion Patek Philippe is the reference in Swiss watchmaking. It is probably the Swiss brand that has most contributed to the excellence of our business. The Patek Philippe Museum in Geneva – which also presents watches from other brands – is the finest horological museum I know. Patek Philippe was my first competitor when I started at Audemars Piguet; and now I have Patek Philippe … not the brand, just the watches! *(Big laugh).* In my collection, I also have Blancpain, Hublot, Omega, Audemars Piguet, Vacheron Constantin, IWC. But as with Yquem in my wine collection, the backbone of my watch collection is from Patek Philippe.

At the Basel Fair in 2014, you chose to wear a 1947 Patek Philippe from your watch collection … with an estimated value of 1 million euros.

That's right. This ended the jealousy between Hublot, TAG Heuer and Zenith as I run these three brands! A classic Patek Philippe from 1947 is timeless!

What is the first watch that you purchased to begin your collection?

Not for my collection, but for my use, the Omega Speedmaster, the watch that went to the moon. This watch was a dream for me: I bought it when I was a student and was earning some money by working at the Post Office. And then, years later, I joined Omega where I rediscovered it!

At first you built your collection on 'coups de coeur' and later more rationally.

As I am someone who enjoys life, I bought mostly with passion: I have trouble buying a piece of history that I do not like. I collect watches that are references in the development of the art of watchmaking. From 1982, I collected Blancpain, and Hublots since 2004. But most of my collection consists of watches made between 1880 and 1980.

Buy to transmit

Today you continue your collection to hand it on, an objective that we know is very important to you.

A collection represents your passion. It is a trace left by its owner. My collections of pictures and cars, like watches and wines reflect some of my passions. My children will inherit, respect, and extend my passions. That's why I collect; if I only did it for me, I would feel that I collected egotistically, and out of vanity.

Which watches do you specifically want to talk about?

I have a sumptuous enamelled Patek Philippe; it is ultra-slim, gold and the enamel quality is exceptional. The subject is beautiful: one side shows the lake of Geneva and the other a boat carrying a cargo of molasses. This watch is the complete representation of Geneva: the city is not only in the subject but the object symbolizes Geneva as the capital of watchmaking, jewellery and enamels.

Sometimes you yourself buy watches that you have offered at a charity auction. I am thinking of an organisation that helps victims of a disease that strikes children

That's right. I buy these Hublot watches for much more than I would have paid for them at the factory. But buying at auction, I acquire purposely to give and share.

I imagine that you never wear these watches but you admire them, especially with those who will inherit your collection.

Most of my watches are in a bank vault but of course from time to time I bring two or three home.

Are you capable of extravagance as a collector?

Yes, my biggest extravagance was buying a Patek Philippe. I bought it at auction as I watched my son play tennis. The phone rang. It was the auctioneer in New York. At every bid I kept saying "yes, yes." And suddenly, there was no one besides me saying yes! But today is one of the watches I'm most proud of and that I regret the least.

17

"Childhood images have bound me to the land which I live today."

Inventing oneself

Luxembourg to Switzerland

Gérard Lelarge: You were born in Luxembourg in 1949. Your great-grandfather was a shoemaker in Luxembourg; he was also the representative of Bally shoes, manufactured in Switzerland. Your father, Jacques, conscripted by the German army in 1942, was forced to fight on the Russian front. On his return in 1946, he took over the family business. Your mother moved to Switzerland when you were ten. What specific memories do you have of those childhood years?

Jean-Claude Biver: I have many memories of Luxembourg where I still have many ties. I also have exceptional memories of our holidays on the Belgian coast where we played in the dunes. I also remember my summer holidays with my brother Marc, staying with our grandparents in Beaujolais. Compared to Luxembourg, Beaujolais was for us almost the south, with another climate, another light and a fabulous landscape. Our grandparents were people of incredible kindness and generosity.

Your father described you as a shy child. He explained that he always had to encourage and reassure you in your projects. It is hard to imagine you being like that…

I was shy when I was younger. But several stages of my life helped me to alleviate my shyness: first my university degree gave me a certain self-respect ("you managed something"); then professional success; finally financial success. So today on a scale of shyness 10, I am at level 2! *(Big burst of laughter.)*

You went to school in Saint-Prex, then the college of Morges. What memories do you have of that period?

During my schooldays, I discovered Lake Geneva, and its swans, ducks, gulls, fog and snow. From my window I could see the Alps, the snow and the lake. Attending this school I started to love this region and began to be tied to it. The mists in spring and in autumn, the green of fir trees are childhood images which for me were highly important. They attracted me and then tied to this land where I live today. These memories have rooted me. They played – and still play – a key role in my balance.

Discover and get to know

After the separation of your parents when you were five, you and your younger brother Marc were put in a boarding school [check that it was a boarding school]. Do you have good memories of this time?

It was a top notch place for privileged children. It had several hectares of grounds on the banks of Lake Geneva. But as beautiful as it was, obviously many students would have preferred to be with their parents: but we were well and truly separated from the family environment. The beauty of the site and the way the children were treated was actually rather pleasant and rewarding for my brother and me. Today, I live 37 kilometers from the institute where I experienced those moments that allowed me to anchor myself here in Switzerland. I then lived with mother near Lausanne, 12 kilometers from the institute. We settled there and no longer wanted to move!

You inherited some of the character traits of your maternal grandfather, Marcel Zeien.

He was a tall, heavily built man, and a great man too: self-willed, hardworking, generous; a sort of patriarch. For all these reasons, I am sometimes compared to him. For us children he always held a fascination and we were very close to him; he also gave us a lot of love. Children love to be with strong and reassuring people because they give them a sense of security. And if in addition these people give a lot of love, for children they become a place of refuge. My brother and I had a chance to experience that gift thanks to our grandfather.

Exploring his passions. All his passions

While enrolled in high school, you worked to earn money and maintain your car, a Beetle. What were your interests and passions? Your adolescence was carefree; you "enjoyed life" as they say.

Yes, I was a sort of hippie. We lived in community; I was living with my best friend, Luc Moudon, today a great doctor, and two girlfriends. We shared out lives: we shared a roof, our resources, and our expenses. In 1968, I was rebellious – I do not say "revolutionary" but "anti-establishment" – and I enjoyed the hippie movement and flower power. I was passionate about nature, skiing, running, sports, and exploring the country (I travelled through Europe, Romania, and Bulgaria in a camper van) … but I had no professional motivation.

Escaping ease

While studying at HEC Lausanne (the Faculty of Business Studies at the University of Lausanne), you worked at the Post Office.

I was working all night, from 8 pm to 5 am: when you are young, you do not need much sleep and you have a lot of strength. Also, I wanted to be financially independent to be able to spend as and when I wanted to. I worked at the Post Office for many years; I enjoyed it and learnt a lot. It also motivated me to continue to study because I realized the hardship and lack of interest of some work. Little by little, I joined professional life: I worked a few weeks in the company Modulo, a company that wanted to compete with Lego and Fisher Price in manufacturing modular toys; then I joined the world of watches at Audemars Piguet.

18

"All you need is love!"

Being a man

The family, source of wealth, peace, love

Gérard Lelarge: As a man you need harmony; and family is the primary source of your balance.

Jean-Claude Biver: For me the family is a source of wealth, peace and love. My clan is made up of three circles. The first circle includes my family, my friends second and third my professional relationships. My family is the most important nucleus. My children and my wife are essential elements of my balance and give me inner peace. In the end, it is this that allows me to be strong.

You personally rub shoulders with celebrities from around the world especially in the context of Hublot partnerships and yet you claim not to be worldly. Hence the importance of your family circle and your house La Poneyre.

I know these people but I do not live among them every day. I am not very social. I'd rather spend the little time that I have on a family evening.

Is this perhaps to protect your privacy?

No, it's simply my preference: sitting on a bench with a local farmer, a glass of Chasselas, watching the mountain and hearing the sound of cowbells on a summer evening gives me more pleasure and satisfaction than strutting around in white tuxedo with a champagne glass in hand at a party for five hundred people. Unless, of course it is an evening with friends.

Always share, respect, forgive

I imagine that your "three commandments" – sharing, respect and forgiveness – are values that you pass to your children.

Not only to my children: I transmit these values to everyone. These values are easy to understand but often difficult to implement: sharing requires continuous effort; as do respect and forgiveness.

Respect is both respect for others and respect for oneself.

All respect begins at home: you cannot respect anyone else, unless you respect yourself. To disrespect someone else, shows a lack of respect for yourself. Sometimes we are a too rigorous in the education of children, so that there is the risk of damaging the respect that the child may have for himself. Our education system should pay more attention to the development of respect for self and others.

You are described as very sensitive, hypersensitive.

I am emotional, very sensitive, sometimes oversensitive; emotions affect me. They are sometimes exaggerated in one way or another; so if I need to make a decision, I have to wait until I cool down.

Are you a strict father?

I was harsh, because I was young and inexperienced. Of course at the time I did not think myself such a bad father. I will give you a simple example: I wanted the kids to play in their room and not to leave their toys lying around in the living room or the dining room; today I am very happy if a child plays next to me, either in my office, in the dining room, in the drawing room, or in the kitchen, because I find that I am enriched by the presence of the child. I find that I have mellowed, I am more attentive to the child, to his needs rather than mine. With age, we tend to have more room for the needs of others. That is why grandparents are often more generous, and more understanding than parents.

You became a grandfather for the first time in 2012.

I have the privilege to be three times a father and once a grandfather. I hope to become a grandfather several times!

All you need is love

You previously defined yourself as a hippie! Can you go back over what may seem like a paradox?

In the 1960s, I was a hippie and beatnik. I was both! The hippie movement was characterized by the slogan *"peace and love"*. At the time the Beatles sang *"All you need is Love."* This movement was the first to be concerned about the protection of nature and respect for animals. The hippie movement was also very romantic, conscious of freedom and the equality of men and women. For me it was the foundation of my ethics and my "three commandments": sharing, respect and forgiveness. I am still a hippie at heart. I may have lost my hippy hair *(Big laugh)* and my extravagant dress sense, but not my romanticism nor my generosity. I remain committed to the respect of nature, animals, others, and oneself. Today I still remain profoundly marked by love.

Love and sharing are essential themes for you.

The only purpose of life is to give love and to transmit it. Thus, the chain of life can continue. Women know this: they give birth through the sharing of their body, sharing their breathing, sharing their blood. Out of this sharing a human being is born; a human being, who in turn requires sharing to mature and to continue life. We are all the result of sharing.

You previously mentioned the two traces that each of us should leave behind. Is this another lesson from the hippie movement?

Yes. The hippie movement especially posed an existential question: "You're 18, you love music but why are you alive? What is the meaning of your life?" My response was to say: "I am leaving two traces, such as those that left by the farmer ploughing his field: one professional furrow and another of love."

Always dare to move forward

You have characterized the sale of Blancpain as positive, yet at the time you perceived it as – I use your words – a "drama", a "terrible wrench." Would you describe yourself as an optimist?

I am convinced that we can always turn a dramatic situation around. This is of course unlike the real dramas – those affecting the family – that are insurmountable; I am thinking for example about the loss of a child. Dramas and professional failures have two sides; hence the importance of focusing on the positive. This attitude is one of the 'springs' that allowed me to bounce back from the sale of Blancpain. I am proactive; therefore inevitably a little optimistic, because the will to do, that is to say, the desire to project to the future is an act of optimism. The entrepreneur is naturally optimistic; were he pessimistic, he would not have the courage to shape his future. If you are very wary about what will happen tomorrow, you will not dare to move forward. But we must dare to go forward. So, be optimistic.

But of course being optimistic does not mean being unrealistic.

We must be able to look at reality. The optimist who has no concept of reality is dangerous. We must constantly take a step back and continually ask ourselves the question: am I going in the right direction?

After selling Blancpain, anxious not to 'betray' it, you remained loyal to the brand for twelve years. You are fundamentally faithful in business and friendship.

I am loyal. I am faithful to my principles, my friends, my love, my passion. I am loyal to the nation, true to the planet. *(To punctuate each point JCB hits the table.)* To respect is to be faithful. Infidelity is a lack of respect, both vis-à-vis the person you are betraying and vis-à-vis yourself.

Living Switzerland's values

You think loyalty is a Swiss trait. What other qualities of your countrymen have you discovered, since you obtained Swiss citizenship in 2011?

The Swiss are hard workers, diligent, precise and creative. Just one example of this creative ingenuity is Nespresso. This subsidiary of Nestlé managed to outdo the Italian espresso and become the reference for coffee. As such, I feel completely Swiss and I am proud of it!

You are committed to the values of your country. What Swiss values are essential for you?

Switzerland's values are those of its citizens. In addition, Switzerland has a political system based on referendum and consensus, not a bi-partisan system of left or right. This prevents the domination of one party over the other. Switzerland is multicultural – we speak four languages – and it is a welcoming haven. Switzerland has one of the best school systems in the world, ranging from the primary school to universities. It is not by chance that in many areas it has the best colleges in the world! It is the same with the medical system. With its cultural tolerance and innovative spirit, the country offers unique opportunities for development for large companies and SMEs. Proof of this can be seen in pharmaceuticals, biotechnology, mechanical engineering, the watch industry, Nestle, etc.

Hublot directly supports small and medium sized industry.

Indeed, we participate in the Swisscom Business Booster competition designed to help SMEs. They are in fact essential to the economy, large groups cannot be built without the network of SMEs.

Distinguish price and value

Your first watch, an Omega, was given to you by your grandfather for your first communion. Can you tell us the story of this watch?

In all good Catholic middle-class families, the godfather, who was often the grandfather, gave a watch at the first communion and at 18, the child wore the watch. So you had a watch for a day – the day of your first Communion – and at 18 a watch for life. Of course, this watch was priceless to me.

And you lost it!

Yes, it was a lack of respect. I did not respect the object properly. I wore my watch when I went skiing; but it was not a watch designed for sports. I was upset about it then and I can still be chagrined about it today, but I saw the benefit to be drawn from that error. I was punished but I have learned a lesson; this mistake made me grow.

Often unfavourable circumstances and negative events help you to change and bounce back.

Error is productive, beneficial. It is only negative if it is repeated. But if the lessons of a first error are learned, we avoid repeating it; that is progress.

About the million-dollar Hublot, you say that this watch symbolizes "competence and excellence." But this watch cannot be pur-

chased by a person with low income and the price represents decades of work.

Whoever buys this watch will have given work to a dozen people for a year. And if that's the case, I hope we sell a lot of these watches. We must not delude ourselves, expensive products, whether in the field of technology or that of luxury, are objects that are not expensive by chance: they are expensive because their labour and production costs are high. What is better: Making objects with 50 cents-worth labour or objects with 500 000 euros-worth of labour? Making these objects with 500 000 euros-worth of labour is preferable since their production involves the use of a large number of workers.

On the subject of luxury that stimulates activity, one is reminded of Voltaire's observation that the superfluous – which we can translate as luxury – was "a very necessary thing." He saw in luxury not only a means of happiness and well-being but also a way to stimulate activity and so benefit others. He wrote: "It is the frivolity and fantasy of men that give a livelihood to the hundred workers I employ and that stimulates industry."

Bravo! That's exactly right. Voltaire understood it all!

Give to others

Would you describe yourself as privileged?

Certainly. First, as I said, to be able make a passion into a profession is a huge privilege. Then I am privileged in terms of family, friends, work, etc. *(At each point, JCB taps the table with his pen.)* When you are as privileged as I am, what do you feel? One has the feeling of an immense injustice: I was born on the right side while billions of human beings for millions of years, were born on the wrong side. As recipients of such privileges, we have a responsibility vis-à-vis others: that of sharing.

Sharing is one of your three commandments. Hence my question: what good causes do you support with your own money?

In particular, I support Action Innocence, founded and directed by Valérie Wertheimer, who fights against paedophilia on the Internet. In my lectures, I do not collect a penny (which allows me to speak freely). But if the organizers have budgets for speakers, I ask them to pay the money to this charity. Personally, I am very sensitive to helping and , sharing.

In this vein you took employees of Blancpain on holiday. Can you tell us more?

That was in 1989. I actually took all the staff at Blancpain on holiday – a hundred employees. We spent a week in October in southern Italy, Naples, Pompeii, and Capri with four history of art professors from the universities of Lausanne and Geneva. So we combined vacation and culture. In the Archaeological Museum of Naples, we could admire the most beautiful miniature mosaics, which are, in a way, similar to watchmaking in their intricacy. I closed the factory to go on holiday with all the staff!

19

"With all that I have been given, I cannot regret, what I did not have."

Living well

Entering the world of sharing

Gérard Lelarge: You have led several companies on an extraordinary journey and today you see your mission as to "transmit".

Jean-Claude Biver: Everyone must pass things on; not only money, but above all ideas, experience, morals, ethics. Privileges are like power or fame; they do not give you rights, but obligations. If one is given a great deal, one must give a great deal.

You explain that "the supreme goal of life is to remain alive after death." What do you mean?

Being alive after his death means "leaving traces." If before leaving you have passed on your love, your knowledge, your experiences, your successes, your failures, your doubts, you can die peacefully: you have given everything . Since, after death, we cannot give much (!) we must give before.

For you, "one who leaves with all that he has, leaves poor." You add: "The most important period of life is … happiness after life." You want to leave two traces: a trace of love and a professional trace.

The trace of love is the most important; Jean d'Ormesson said if you managed to leave a trace of love, 95 % of your life has been successful. I fully share this vision of success. If possible one should also leave a second trace; in exercising your profession; so that your journey was useful.

You explain: "When we are young, we live for the future. When you are fulfilled, you live for the future of others, the future of your children." This thought can apply to the collections that you have made: watches, wine, pictures and cars. You explain that through these collections, some part of you will remain alive after your death.

In addition to my collection of watches and wine, I do have a collection of paintings – especially the Impressionists and the Fauves: I am very sensitive to colors – and a collection of vintage cars. But I'm not a collector who hoards, I am a collector who consumes. I wear the watches, I drive the cars, I drink the wine. Collecting encourages me to share not to keep for myself. In addition, I have the desire to leave a trace of my passions to my children. This is how I make sense of collecting.

Never stop

According to you, "there is a time to learn, a time to do, a time to impart and a time to depart." In late 2011, you transferred the operational management of Hublot to Ricardo Guadalupe but you remain president of the board. Early 2014 you were appointed chairman of LVMH's watchmaking division. Do you really want to work until you are 75 years old as you announced?

I have to see until what age I remain young. As long as the mind is curious, and learns, one remains young. For me, no longer being young is to have no curiosity, to believe we know and do not learn. About my new responsibilities at LVMH, I would say it is a "final sprint to the finish." I always thought when I was running marathons if my last kilometre was the fastest of the 42 kilometres then I had managed my resources and effort well and I finished with pleasure rather than pain.

It's the same for my professional marathon. The last three or five years of my career should be fuller and busier. I was extremely happy, honoured and motivated when I agreed to become president of the watch division of LVMH until the end of 2019 at least.

Do you have personal or professional regrets?

With all that I have received, I cannot regret the little I did not have. When you have been spoiled by life, you must say thank you and have no regrets.

That said, if I had a dream – a dream is not a regret – that would be for my children tell me one day in five years: "Come on, let's make a Biver watch. We will work like crazy and you, the patriarch, give us a couple of instructions and above your blessing." Creating a Biver watch is a chapter of my life that could have been opened fifteen, twenty, maybe even ten years ago: but much less likely today as I approach 70, as I do not see myself starting all over again!

What do you expect from this book?

If a person, only one, manages to be inspired and remember a few lines of this book, then we have already succeeded! And this book will have been worth doing. Again, my goal is to share, transmit, especially to young entrepreneurs, some principles of behaviour and management and of a few rules that I think may be useful.

What thoughts should the reader take away?

Three thoughts:

First thought: Look to your passion and you will find it.

Second thought: Do not go with the flow, explore new territories.

Third thought: Give love, you will remain alive after death.

20

„Proust Questionnaire"

Your greatest personal successes

My children, my family and my ethics, which I was able to maintain against all odds. And also having managed to turn my passion into work.

Your biggest personal failures

A divorce, but it was a failure that allowed me to bounce back and create a second trace of love.

Your best memory as a business leader

The holiday in 1989 I gave to all the Blancpain staff with whom I spent a week in the south of Italy.

Your worst memory as entrepreneur

When I had to announce the sale of Blancpain. It was an irrational sale, one that I regretted for years, until the birth of Pierre, my second son, and until the beginning of my adventure with Hublot.

Your best memory as a man

The birth of my children. Despite the progress of science, birth remains a miracle, a miracle of perfection, beauty and hope; a miracle of love.

Your worst memory as a man

2016 the death of my father!

Your greatest fears

The health of my children.

What you would you like your friends say about you?

That I was generous and honest. Generosity is a form of love and honesty is a form of ethics. I would like to leave a memory of love and righteousness.

What would you like your enemies say about you?

The same thing!

Your greatest betrayal

Fortunately I have not got one, because I hate betrayal.

How others see you?

Some see me loyal, faithful, generous and honest. Others speak badly of me and see me with, jealousy and envy; the latter allow me to measure my professional success.

The reasons why you are sometimes annoying

I occupy space and I talk a lot. Sometimes I try to dominate and direct.

The fashion you find most ridiculous

None, because I'm open to everything and able to understand even what I do not like.

What revolts you?

Lying and injustice.

What annoys you?

Jargon and empty words.

What hurts you?
Cant and Demagoguery

What amuses you?
To work, discover, learn.

What attracts you?
Generosity and fidelity.

The entrepreneur whom you would most like to resemble
Steve Jobs has changed the destiny of the objects he created, such as the camera phone or music player.

The politician whom you would most like to resemble
Churchill.

The Creator or artist whom you would like to resemble
Picasso said: "We need a long time to become young." I find that extraordinary: youth is spontaneity, creativity, naivety, curiosity. For me, to be young after a certain age is the real success.

What would you like God to say to you in welcoming you to paradise?
"Welcome. But you were so good on earth, I allow you to go back. I will not keep you this time. Come back later." *(Great bursts of laughter.)*

Are you a believer?
Yes and no. I believe in love. When one believes in love, one is close to God and religion since all believers say their god is love. They also say that their god is eternal; and love is also eternal. I believe in eternal love; the love we give never dies; it leaves an indelible mark.

Your main character trait

I am both fragile and strong. If I have a particular weakness it is that I am very emotional and I react much with the heart. But I have strength because I want to create and the challenge motivates me.

The character trait of which you are least proud

I like excess and I tend to be excessive.

Your cult books and films

I love *The Little Prince, The Fables of La Fontaine, Modern Times* and the films of Alfred Hitchcock.

Your favourite composers

Chopin and the Beatles.

Your favourite painters

The Fauves and the Impressionists because I am in love with colour. Colour attracts me, it makes me dream, it gives me hope.

Your favourite drink

Red wine, of all regions, because wine is part of the culture of the land. But my favourite is the red Bordeaux, Château Cheval Blanc.

Your favourite cigarettes

I smoke a few cigars; five or six per year.

Your favourite foods

Coq au vin, mashed potatoes, fondue, snails, frogs, crayfish.

The talent you wish you had

To play music.

The faults to which you are most indulgent

Vanity. The entrepreneur is sometimes too greedy and too conceited. But I learned how to forgive.

How would you like to die?

Rich, that is to say, having returned everything as regards love, knowledge, experiences, and vision. And leaving traces of my passions through my collections. Dying poor means having nothing to return.

Your daily motto

Loyalty, honesty, righteousness.

Your motto in the business world

Always be first, different and unique.

What you listen in your car?

News.

The object you cannot do without

My computer.

The wallpaper on your computer screen

My son wishing me happy birthday.

What would you have said instead of Neil Armstrong?

I could not have said it better.

The place you love above all

My house.

Your favourite landscape

The one around my home in Switzerland and around my home in Ramatuelle.

Your favourite journey

Going home.

The most famous person in your phone book

Bernard Arnault.

The two names that you recently removed from your phonebook

Happily no one.

What would you change about your character if you could?

I have a little more patience.

What would you change about your physique if you could?

I would like to be slimmer; which would make it easier to climb mountain passes on my bike!

What do you have that is in bad taste?

My sweaters with holes.

The gift you give most often

Wine, because it is the gift of communion.

The gift you do not like – or would not like – to receive

I like to get all gifts.

Your greatest extravagance

The purchase of a Patek Philippe. But this is one of watches which I am most proud of and that I regret the least.

The criticism that most affects you

Lies. I hate lies.

The criticism to which you are indifferent

Those which come from slanderers, those who are envious, and jealous. But in fact, I love them because they are a measure of my success!

The compliments to which you are most sensitive

Those made to my children and my wife.

The compliments that leave you indifferent

Those made to me that are neither sincere nor justified.

21

The 15 Golden Rules of Jean-Claude Biver

The rules of life

Share, respect, forgive
Have the courage to be wrong and accept failure
Build strong personal relationships
Learn, again and again
Never give up your DNA

The management rules

Invest yourself totally
Know with whom to surround yourself and whom to listen to
Always conquer, don't be happy just to direct
Behave like a guerrilla
Act like a *"winner"*, whatever the circumstances

The marketing rules

Always be first, different and unique
Tell stories, that make others dream
Innovate in tradition
Anticipate your customers needs
Endure by rising above fashions

Epilogue

Knowing the man

The expression is probably both presumptuous and inaccurate. Do hours – even a great many hours – of conversation around my tape recorder and in front of the cameras of Hublot TV really allow one to "know" JCB, the extraordinary character both as leader and man?

I must disclose immediately that my view is at least partly distorted by my liking for my subject, which emerged on our first meeting. I was also charmed by the natural way he spoke during our interviews. So, I deliver a partially subjective portrait, that is personal and based in particular on details that touched me. Among them is a memory of our second meeting in Paris: Jean-Claude Biver noticed the watch I wear. "This is the watch belonged to one of my wife's grandfathers." "These watches there are the most beautiful," he replied. Another detail that touched me was that despite obvious differences in status and career, I discovered we have two things in common. First the love and reverence that we both have for our maternal grandfathers from whom we inherited certain traits and memories of happy childhood spent with them. Then, the importance attached to the first communion watch that these grandfathers gave us… although not having lost mine, I still wear it.

Beyond these facts that probably seem anodyne to many of you, how does one define JCB? Several adjectives can be used to characterize him. Jean-Claude Biver is naturally warm and charismatic, pragmatic and bold, and deeply human … in other words complicated.

JCB is naturally warm and charismatic

Three weeks after our meeting at the Wine Business Club, I received an email: "Thanks for the idea of the book project. I like it very much. I can't wait to get started on it with you!" What wonderful encouragement to give the best of oneself. The man remains the same when the microphone is switched off and the cameras have stopped running: simple, attentive, open. We lunch in the conference room next to his office facing the magnificent view of the Vaud landscape and the lake. We discuss the political situation in France, we talk about our children. He recalls his first granddaughter, Paloma, "Paloma is dove," he notes with a smile.

He is evidently a man who has mastered the art of speaking and his charisma is evident whether one-to-one or in front of the audiences at his lectures. He also has a gift for humour. "When we sleep, we do no wrong, even if we are bad. When they wake up, bad people, they become dangerous. When they sleep, there is nothing to fear, they are not making mischief. From time to time, we are happy that people are asleep …" is just one example Michel Audiard would not have disowned this little speech that Jean-Claude Biver ends with a big laugh.

Along with sharing his values, JCB has an innate sense of teaching, through simple examples and a way with words, that hits the bull's eye. In his lectures, he focuses on the simplicity and authenticity of his remarks. He knows better than anyone the importance of non-verbal communication right up to taking the stage at the traditional désalpe in September and wearing the 'bredzon' the traditional work clothes of the Alpine cowherd.

JCB is pragmatic and bold

His pragmatism can be easily measured by his results as an entrepreneur; an entrepreneur who in recent years revived Omega, revived Blancpain and gives an extraordinary impetus to transforming Hublot, transforming turnover into net profit in a year! The press hail him as "an outstanding figure of the Swiss watch industry" and describe him as "visionary businessman", and "excellent strategist". The list of awards and honours that he has received is impressive.

And this thanks to original principles, often opposed to what is taught in business school. Jean-Claude Biver explains that he has read very few management books, but he has written one: the one you have in your hands, which can be used to guide many entrepreneurs and seasoned executives looking for recipes that work. It offers unconventional advice, for example find the creativity of children, always aim to be "first, different and unique." It assumes an audacity that is sometimes lacking in the business world where copying is more comfortable than innovating. It assumes an iconoclastic approach, for example wanting to sell Blancpain watches without showing them as was the case in Basel fair in 1984. It assumes the audacity to provoke, but not just for the sake of provocation; there must be substance behind the provocation. Thus, JCB brought cows to the Place Vendôme for the inauguration of the Hublot store to remind everyone that the origin of the Swiss watch is in farming. For him, the successful entrepreneur must be a "guerrilla" who dares, who goes off the beaten track, who does not hesitate to surprise his rivals and who knows how to seize opportunities.

The audacity of ignoring the naysayers: who said that investing in football is an aberration for a luxury business and, unaware that the world is not limited to France or even Europe, choked when they saw the "sulphurous" Maradona, who is very popular in Asia, become a Hublot partner. The audacity to create a real big bang, the name particularly well chosen to symbolize the change Hublot introduced into the world of luxury watches by connecting the past and the future, by using a sandwich construction to making watches!

Ever the original entrepreneur, JCB says that his best friend is doubt. He sees failure as the "only way to access success": "When we are children, it is our falls and our tears that allow us to gradually find the best way to move forward." More than just contrary positions to charm an audience that is already converted, these management principles can be, and indeed are, applied in everyday life. "When I receive a CV, I am naturally attracted to candidates who failed. In fact, always look for positive energy in the negative. Life is always the *yin* and *yang*, day and night, hot and cold, water and earth."

JCB is deeply human … so complex

The boss of Hublot often refers to his "three commandments" (share, respect, forgive), as relatives of those principles that Confucius stated around two and a half thousand years ago, when he advocated that his followers act with humanity and behave as the good man distinguished by his virtue, the exercise of his talents and his morality.. Jean-Claude Biver stresses the need to leave two traces: a professional trace and trace of love. "The only purpose of life is to give love and to transmit it. Thus the chain of life can continue," he says.

How much 'spin' is there in his words? If as we know JCB has mastered communication techniques, can we therefore suspect him of deceiving his audience? No. "I'm not an actor, I do not play any role." Jean-Claude Biver is not content to mouth generous principles, he put them into practice through personal philanthropic actions and behaviour in daily life. If the man is not genuine explain how he has had a team of loyal follows the last thirty years?

JCB, a big boss, defines himself as a guerrilla businessman, as we have seen, but also as a hippie! What does such a provocative statement mean? Even if he says: "Of course a hippie who has evolved" he honestly seems committed to respect his fellow man, respect nature, respect the connections between people, and respect the importance of love. With an ethic grounded in love and applied both to his work and to his private life, Jean-Claude Biver lives in harmony. The family is essential for his balance. Gregarious, JCB is not a loner; he loves and needs to be surrounded by people.

While many leaders face media criticism – sometimes unfounded – almost all articles devoted to the boss of Hublot are eulogies … and, in the"worst" cases, neutral. Does he want unanimous approval? No, of course not. Remember what delights JCB and lights up his eyes: "I love those who badmouth me, those who are envious and jealous. I love them because they are the barometer of my success!" The man leaves nothing unsaid. His outspokenness is plain, for example with regard to the Church which speaks "as if we were still living in the Middle Ages" or politicians – who "too often lack vision, charisma, courage, honesty". To those who describe the price of a Hublot watch as what a humble employees earns over many years of work, he asks: "What is better: making objects with 50 cents-worth of labour or objects with 500 000 euros-worth of labour leading to the employment of many?"

Jean-Claude Biver is capable of self criticism; he acknowledges being talkative, taking up space, dominating and leading the group, sometimes being exaggerated and excessive. He confides that he reads few books when so many big bosses pride themselves on culture: "I'm not an intellectual; I am a pragmatist," he says, almost apologetically – passionate pragmatist who at the end of 2012 received the Hommage a la passion award from the Fondation de la Haute Horlogerie in Geneva .

The man is naturally optimistic. For him, life is a daily reward, and with it the chance exercise his passion to create, initiate, innovate. But JCB also admits "to telling the truth with a little paint." So, bad memories such as the separation of her parents, his own divorce or the sale of Blancpain are presented as opportunities to bounce back, even if these memories bear the watermark of regrets. Let us recall the boarding school where Jean-Claude and Marc were sent after the divorce of their parents: "As beautiful as it was, many students would have preferred to be with their parents: we were well and truly separated from the family environment." Jean-Claude Biver is also well and truly thin-skinned as he readily acknowledges. He cried on the day of the sale of Blancpain to Nicolas Hayek, a day when he "believed that the world would collapse"… but he corrects himself and adds: "Finally the wrench of losing Blancpain turned into something extraordinarily positive." He concludes: "I cry with one eye and laugh the other."

Turning to the past JCB explains: "I have zero – zero – zero – zero regret" and adds: "All I did always ended up well for me." A psychoanalyst might see in such words proof of denial. Or simply part of the Cou method for moving forward?

It is evident that the man is passionate, needs new challenges after each victory. Drawing a self-portrait without saying as much, JCB cites the example of the mountaineer who, having reached the summit of Everest, says 'never again' but is off again six months later, when he has treated his frostbite.

If the Hublot boss likes to quote Picasso, I too would choose a quote from Picasso, in my opinion, it sums up Jean-Claude Biver, both leader and man, and both intensely passionate "It is your work in life, that is the ultimate seduction."

Acknowledgements

I must first thank Jean-Claude Biver, who showed his full confidence in my project and who, through his availability and his enthusiastic commitment, enabled me to complete it.

I also want to thank all employees of Hublot with whom I have been in contact during the writing of this book and especially Alexia Erb, Kari Palaz, Rose Christen and Joan Dominguez for both their efficiency and the warmth of their welcome.

Gérard Lelarge